Gyan Yoga

Richa Tilokani, who holds a Master's degree in Business Administration (MBA) from SP Jain Institute of Marketing & Research, Mumbai, is an author and poet who started out as a marketing and advertising professional.

Her first book, *The Teachings of Bhagavad Gita,* was nominated by the PragatiE Vichaar Literature Fest 2022 in the Best Debut Non-Fiction book category. Her second book, *7 Lessons of Karm Yoga* (2024), was shortlisted in the Best Self-Help book category at the PragatiE Vichaar Literature Fest 2025 and was also nominated in the Popular Choice category at the AutHer Awards 2025. Her third book *Game. Set. Match: Krishna's Teachings for Kids* was released in 2024.

Gyan Yoga

Knowledge, Acceptance,
Identity, Truth

Richa Tilokani

RUPA

First published by
Rupa Publications India Pvt. Ltd 2025
161-B/4, Gulmohar House,
Yusuf Sarai Community Centre,
New Delhi 110049

Sales centres:
Bengaluru Chennai
Hyderabad Kolkata Mumbai

P-ISBN: 978-93-7003-757-1
E-ISBN: 978-93-7003-782-3

First impression 2025

10 9 8 7 6 5 4 3 2 1

Printed in India

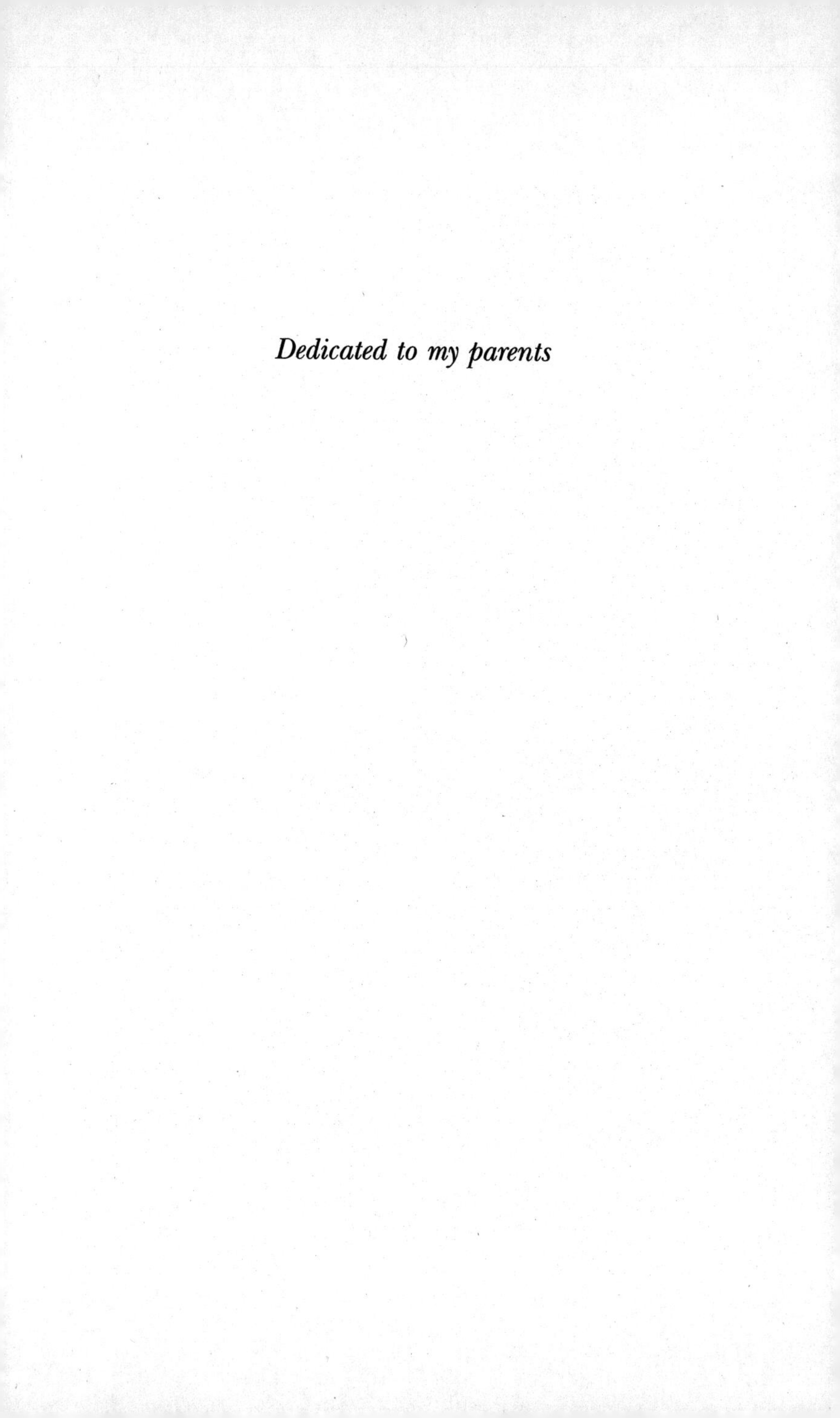

Dedicated to my parents

Na hi gyanena sadrisham pavitramiha vidyate
Tat svayam yogasamsidhah kaalenatmani vindati
(BG 4:38)

There is nothing as sublime or pure as transcendental knowledge. It is the mature fruit of mysticism and the devoted enjoy it within the self.

Contents

Contents

PART A

Introduction to Gyan Yoga: A Journey of Evolution

Since the beginning of time, carbon-based life forms have been on a never-ending journey of evolution. The primordial soup which led to their birth contained the building blocks of life in perfect proportion; they began as single-celled organisms that eventually evolved into multi-cellular animals, birds and human beings. This process unfolded over millions of years—some species perished along the way, while others persisted, developing unique features and skillsets to navigate the harsh and inhospitable terrain of the still volatile earth.

Amongst all species, the most astounding progress was made by our ancestors who evolved into modern-day Homo sapiens. It played out slowly but surely, as more intelligent species replaced the earlier, less-evolved ones.

One thing was common between them all. Be it the Homo habilis who crafted tools from stone and organic materials, or the creative Neanderthals who dwelled in dark caves and painted on their walls, or those who came before and after them, or the Homo sapien who now dwells online—each group persevered against heavy odds.

And while doing so, don't you think these disparate groups, some flourishing concurrently while others separated by years and processes of evolution, would have gazed up at the night sky dotted with twinkling stars, and pondered over the big questions of life, same as we do today? For it is in our nature to look for and crave answers, which throw light on why things are the way they are.

From an anthropological, philosophical and spiritual aspect, we have always been brimming with questions: who are we, what is our identity, how did we come here, were we created by God, what is His nature, what is ours and what is our raison d'etre on this giant piece of rock that is suspended in a swirling galaxy of millions of shimmering stars, planets, meteors and asteroids, in a never-ending, never-beginning universe, manifesting and un-manifesting since time immemorial.

We are perpetually haunted by the whys, whats and hows of these questions, so you can imagine how bewildering they must have been for the firsts of our kind. Perhaps, the primitive hunter gatherer would have reviled and respected in equal measures the tempestuous, mysterious nature of the universe and struggled with its inscrutability and unpredictability.

On one hand, he would have been grateful for the bounty it offered, but on the other hand, would have cowered in his cave dwelling when nature unleashed its savage fury in the form of deadly earthquakes, violent volcanic eruptions, incessant floods, devastating droughts and torrential downpour.

However he did manage to thrive, the ferocious forces

of nature notwithstanding. The domestication of animals, development of agriculture, creation of communities, tools and implements enhanced his chances of survival in the bleak, often unforgiving environment.

Still, his evolutionary streak and thirst for exploration continued to grow unabated and led him to mount daring expeditions with varying degrees of success. And today it can rightfully be said that he did succeed in taming and mapping the wild, wild world; the inexplicable unknown is now the fairly well-known.

Modern man continues to break new ground, be it in the sciences, quantum physics, medicine, technology and artificial intelligence, pushing the boundaries of progress. So much has been achieved but they want so much more—to do more, to grow more, to create more, to win more.

From being the hunted, they have become the hunters. No longer do they cower in caves—now, they rule all they survey. Their eyes are trained on the horizon; having conquered the Earth, they now seek to conquer the universe, the multiverse, and everything that lies within and beyond.

So, what inspires this relentless zeal in them, in us and the hardy groups who flourished before us and the ones that will succeed us?

The will to survive. The thirst for more.

This is why even after centuries of growth, we are in search of 'more'; exploring, discovering, bubbling with questions, searching for answers and longing to learn, grow, prosper, conquer and expand, to go where no one has dared to go before, and to add to the individual and social reservoir of wisdom.

Our mind-body is designed to do exactly that: it is steadily processing information, evolving, adapting and changing. Why? Well, it is hardwired to survive in extreme conditions. An engineering marvel, its billions of cells function in sync by asking questions, exchanging information and energy, relaying answers, directing resources and working in harmony with not only itself, but every other element of the universe. No other creation of nature comes close to it in terms of perfection, grace or complexity.

But is the mind-body a mere machine? Like an evolved computer crammed with data, information, statistics and facts?

No, certainly it is not just a collection of the lungs, liver, bones, skin and kidney. Unlike crusty machines, it possesses something elemental that makes it greater than the sum of its parts.

An X factor.

Here, I am not referring to the social networking site Twitter or to plain old curiosity, which is indeed a force to reckon with. What I am referring to is a factor deeper, mystical and embedded in the soul, rooted in reality and truth which propels growth, drives evolution and has the potential to usher in a new era of renaissance.

The knowledge factor—a divine dimension of existence

This mysterious X is the knowledge factor, the perpetual drive to imbibe knowledge, which makes us greater than the supposed sum of the parts. It is what makes us human, what has empowered us to reach the top of the food chain and allowed us to progress in several aspects over millennia, while other species languished, or worse still, vanished from the face of the earth.

It is this primordial factor which empowers us to transform, translate and transcend the constraints of the cosmos and space-time. A fundamental portal to the higher self and a sacred gateway to social, cultural, emotional and spiritual progress, it is an essential, evolutionary component of nature.

Yes, knowledge, wisdom, logic and rational thought, they inform the evolutionary instinct which defines humanness and also allow one to exceed the said humanness—bestowing a form of a stunning superpower transcending the frailties and follies of the flesh.

We survive, learn, grow, and evolve because it is the cardinal rule of life—because we must, because we know no other way, because it is the path forward. As individuals and as societies, we are geared to reject any form of stagnation or backsliding, the antonyms of growth. Indeed, it is the plateauing of progress which portends the eventual death of the intellect, halts the advance of the community and poses an existential threat to the world.

'What comprises this so-called knowledge factor?' one may wonder.

Well, the English dictionary defines this factor as facts, information or skill acquired through experience or through education, or a theoretical or practical understanding of a subject.

However, the ancient Indian sages and philosophers celebrated the knowledge factor as the base of the universe, the community and the individual. They divided it into two broad groups:

- *Apara Vidya* or Material knowledge: It is the basic wisdom required to navigate the family, workplace, community and nation. It includes the entire creation—all the beings, the mind, the ego and the natural elements—fire, water, air, earth and ether.
- *Para Vidya* or Higher knowledge: It is an elevated insight into the *para prakriti* or higher nature which ensures self-realization and liberation.

Apara vidya is the route to fulfilling one's potential while para vidya is the advanced form of knowledge existing beyond the binaries of the material world. Due to its abstruse nature, it was and still is considered out of bounds for the lay person. But a healthy balance of both material and para awareness is a must to comprehend the nature of both the self and the cosmos.

Now, how can both be acquired?

Origin of Gyan Yoga: Ancient roots. Boundless wisdom

By the honourable path of Gyan Yoga, the dedicated pursuit of knowledge which nurtures, illuminates and guides one towards the highest self.

An ancient treasure trove of wisdom, Gyan Yoga or the art of knowledge traces its profound roots back to the Bhagavad Gita, believed to have been compiled more than 5000 years ago. Its seminal tenets were revealed by Lord Krishna to the Pandava prince Arjuna on the battlefield of Kurukshetra in the northern part of the Indian subcontinent. This path of peace and prosperity also finds mention in the sacred texts of Sanatana Dharma like the Upanishads, the Vedas and the Puranas.

Gyan Yoga approaches the goal of existence, the essence of creation, the true identity of man, the core of all identities and lustrous truths with an analytical and philosophical bent of mind. Although contemporary society is unaware of its importance and relevance, steeped as it is in the chaos and conflict of materialism, it is not merely a path of growth but a calling which may be delayed, but never denied, for—

Knowledge is the journey of the soul,
The language of the heart,
The flow of time eternal,
The whirl of star and space,
The tapestry of generations,
The wealth of ancestors,
The window to the past, present and future.

Indivisible, it rises to humble the skies.
Inevitable, it stands through the storms of night.

Eternal, it moves at the speed of light
Boundless, it expands to encompass the universe.
Beyond the body and beyond the mind,
It dwells in the realm of the divine
Enduring, eternal, equable, ever-lasting,
It is the expression of the sacred
And the call of the Self.

This book offers a brief introduction to Gyan Yoga and discusses its six key tenets and their relevance and application in the current age of division and artificial intelligence.

Nature of higher knowledge: Authentic, abundant, accepting

Material knowledge has multiple origins and is multi-faceted, dependent on external sources, all of which are finite in nature. For example, knowledge of physics, chemistry, biology, art and architecture is finite in nature and can be mastered with the assistance of books, courses and subject matter experts.

However, pure knowledge is an enriching and unending saga of authenticity, abundance and acceptance with a single yet indivisible, interminable, inexhaustible source. It is a cosmic quest for collective and individual liberation, forged in the blaze of self and divine realization. Rich with meaning, purpose and life, its mystical nature is described as follows:

- **It possesses a singular, overarching source:** This source may be referred to as God, Self, universe, *Atman, Brahman,* Divine or higher knowledge. Whichever the worldly label, the transcendent source remains singular and universal. For example, take the sacred Ganga River. It originates at Gomukh at the base of the Gangotri glacier in the craggy Himalayas in Uttarakhand, popularly known as the Devbhumi or the land of the Gods. It begins as the gushing headstream Bhagirathi and embarks on an epic voyage across the terrains of India, travelling 2525 km. Along the way, it is embraced by meandering streams and tropical tributaries, but they do little to alter its core identity and origin. While some worship it as a divine incarnation, others see it as merely a body of water—and still others treat it as nothing more than a place to discharge effluents. Is it all of these, or none of them?
- In Bengal, Ganga splits into two streams, Padma and Hooghly, before it pours itself into the turbulent waters of the Bay of Bengal. Now has it become the bounteous Ganga, the youthful Bhagirathi, the sacred Hooghly or the bubbly Padma? The answer may depend on which place you are standing in and who you pose the question to. However, the divine river's original identity remains unchanged, irrespective of the location. A changing perception does not alter its true source or nature. Similarly, higher knowledge

flows across the length and breadth of humanity, across the shadow and light of life, across the dawn and dusk of hope, but its revered identity and source remain singular and indivisible.

- **It resides within the spiritual essence:** The pursuit of Gyan Yoga may unfold across national and emotional boundaries, over rugged mountains and glassy rivers, down the slopes of verdant valleys and into the heart of lush farmlands. But at any given moment, the spiritually desired awareness exists within. This should make the learning process fairly straight-forward. All we have to do is search the depths of our, soul and we will arrive at the desired confluence? But this rigorous process of analysis includes discarding the cloak of ignorance and accepting the authentic identity, which may require a complex transformative journey and sometimes, multiple births.
- **It is not obtained** by merely reading the scriptures (although that may help to some extent), listening to lectures or podcasts, or repeating lines spouted by god-men. Rather, it is imbibed by the sheer grace of divinity. When practised, it is referred to as higher knowledge but when not imbibed and shared, it remains in information form.
- **It offers the sweet fruit of unabating freedom:** It is a sacred calling which releases oneself from the bondage of desire, ego and materialism, ensuring a life of peace and purpose. It leads to the summit

of freedom-liberation from the never-ending painful cycle of birth, death and rebirth.

- **It drives authenticity:** That which empowers, which allows the fulfilment of potential and the achievement of the collective goal is described as the authentic path of knowledge. Its foundational light bestows a direction of holistic growth and a life of courage to the advanced seeker.
- **It is infinite:** Never does it end, never does it begin; never does it cease, never does it pause. The unifying awareness of this transcendent path of knowledge extends in every direction, across portals, across space-time. One may wonder—where is it present? The counter question is: when and where is it *not* present? Yet only the fortunate, the blessed, and the determined succeed in tasting its sweet nectar.
- **It is eternal:** It is not created or destroyed as that would imply a period of void when it did not exist, which is inconceivable. The words 'creation' or 'destruction' are considered irrelevant to this path; it has existed since the genesis of time and will continue to exist in the future. In the past, present and future, it is and will remain vibrant, germane and grounded in eternity.
- **It ensures the acceptance of life's truths**, which release the material mind from the bondage of sorrow and illusion, brightening and elevating the individual and social consciousness.
- **It has a divine origin** and comprehending its

elevated nature is akin to understanding the essence of existence.

- **It belongs to all** nationalities, people, castes, creed, religions and sects and is evident in the abundance of love, bliss, devotion, excellence, growth, peace and compassion. It is not an indulgence or luxury, but a necessity and birth-right of humanity.

Why pursue Gyan Yoga: Navigating the digital and daily wilderness

However, you may wonder, why should one seek knowledge, whether higher or material? Why pursue wisdom, rational thought and logic so intently? With plenty of yogas in the market including beer yoga, goat yoga (!), hot yoga, sleeping (in the literal sense) yoga, sweat yoga, aerial yoga, why do I require yet another form, that too Gyan Yoga?

This is because in the absence of higher knowledge, we risk drifting towards ignorance and materialism, towards division and destruction, towards war and violence. And the further we will move away from the quintessential source, the further we will be from a life of abundance, progress, acceptance, awareness, compassion, tolerance and gratitude. The greater the distance, the further we will be from sustainable progress, from success and from the natural laws of life.

So what? What we don't know won't hurt us. In Hindi, there is a saying which explains this line of thought: *aankh muh bandh, toh sab changa* (If you avoid the inconvenient, things will appear fine). It is escapism at its finest, a sorry mode of avoiding the blinding glare of the harsh realities of life. But the crushing weight of reality will not cease to make its presence felt, if we do not choose to make its acquaintance.

The solution is not to turn a blind eye and luxuriate in oblivion—doing so leaves us vulnerable to the destructive forces of ignorance. Instead, we must pursue intelligent engagement and thoughtful exploration.

That is because ignorance is not bliss, although you may have heard otherwise.

Down the rabbit hole of ignorance or *maya*: The poisonous pivot of modern times

Unsustainable and unaffordable ignorance is one of the root causes of problems in the age of artificial intelligence. This is ironic because one of the key objectives of rapid digitalization was to bring the world closer in a holistic sense by eradicating ignorance.

Instead, it has mutated into a slow-release poison which corrodes the mind, infects intellect, weakens resolve, gnaws away at communities and vitiates the national fabric—an intimidating creature with vicious tentacles which entrap the gullible, its unceasing power threatens social peace, prosperity, cohesion and the rise of the collective consciousness.

It may be a luxury for the high and mighty but is an epitome of brutality for the masses, and in all likelihood, they are pretending to be ignorant for their vested interests.

Ignorance often begins at a subtle starting point—but grows into an insidious and ruthless enemy which we may underestimate at our own peril. Perhaps you, too, believe it is toothless and can be safely ignored? At first glance, it does appear to be as benign as a pebble, but what if it is hurled onto a serene pond? That humble pebble has the potential to disturb the hitherto tranquil surface of the water body.

Try it out yourself. Toss a pebble into a pond and observe the ripples cascading out in all directions.

When alone and at rest, it cannot accomplish much, but when it ingratiates itself into another space, its pessimistic energy can and does blight that landscape. If one pebble has such power, imagine what a truckload of dusty pebbles can achieve? If all the sharp, dirty, rough pebbles launch an onslaught, the cerulean pond will become uncontrollably turbulent, its waters will witness turmoil and its marine life will be disturbed.

Now let's try to relate the not-so-serene pond to the not-so-serene contemporary society. Obviously, there is an array of pointy pebbles at work here. They are the various forms of materialism which generate ripples of disquiet and division, stress and sorrow, hate and hostility.

The echo chamber of social media

It must be acknowledged that social media has vastly contributed to the worsening of the social climate. It has generated an unchecked number of sharp pebbles along with an echo chamber of ignorance, from where disquiet and mayhem flow in all directions.

Here, unsurprisingly, lies and rumors go viral with ease and trumped-up claims or blame games victimize and ruin reputations. Traveling across e-grapevines at lightning speed, they fan the hungry flames of hatred and generate unrest among public, affecting inter-community and inter-personal relations.

Who checks the genuineness of the source when they can instantly react?

The impact is catastrophic. No wonder, the online and offline worlds are drowning in various forms of ignorance including fake news, superstitions, misinformation efforts, deep fakes, rumour mongering, hate campaigns, Twitter bots and statements of omission and commission. Phew. Have all of us not witnessed some or maybe all of them in action?

Still believe the pebble is harmless? Or is it a boulder picking up speed and size?

If such forms of ignorant pebbles continue to increase in size, volume and frequency and sources of knowledge dissipate or are ignored, it will lead to rampant unrest and division. We still cannot comprehend the full scale of horrors they can inundate us with.

Already, we have witnessed elections manipulated, facts distorted, communities provoked, and blatant campaigns orchestrated to advance a post-truth, post-reality narrative. The anti-immigrant riots in towns across United Kingdom in August 2024 are a case in point, wherein far-right violence targeted innocent victims on the basis of false viral posts. Another example is the horrifying spike in gender violence across the nation and the rise in cases of disturbances and unrest across the world. And what about the casualty in these cases: the victim, the truth? It is often suppressed, forgotten and buried under the weight of falsehoods. A travesty of justice, indeed.

The system is further weighed down by the absence of genuine leaders, resulting in myriad forms of injustice, insecurity, division, bigotry and polarization.

Quietly, everyone is alarmed at the rise of this nameless, faceless malignant *avidya* or *maya* which threatens to push the collective intellect into a well of darkness and destruction. As it rules with an iron fist, it manipulates the educated, evolved man and the leaders who ironically do not know how to lead. Clearly, ignorance is the precursor to hatred and hostility, division and downturn, insecurity and instability which are inimical to the social, financial, spiritual and intellectual progress of the individual and the collective.

Violence begets violence: The hubris of man

Let's examine a hallmark of and a by-product of ignorance—the explosion of violence in a country which considers itself the steward of the free world. Yes, I am referring to the largest economy in the world, the United States of America which boasts of a GDP (Gross Domestic Product) of 20 trillion dollars. And yes, I am referring to the sad epidemic of mass shootings which have come to define its social landscape.

According to the Centre for Disease Control and Prevention (CDC), in 2023, 48,830 people lost their lives to gun-related injuries in the United States—a staggering, sobering figure for such a powerful nation, especially over such a short span of time. And that's not all, these statistics are worsening each year. If even their president Donald Trump can be shot at, then what hope and security can the common man hope to possess? Still, frantic efforts to control the sale of weapons are stymied by many a politician backing the arms lobby.

These vociferous supporters of gun ownership profess guns don't kill, which leaves us with the other element in the equation: people. So, they are the problem? Wonder how that can be addressed? It does not require sleuthing skills to solve this mystery. As per the nature of man, if we hand over a gun to a person, they will use it.

But gun supporters invoke the right to self-defence. And sure, people do have that right. But are they really expecting entire armies to break into their homes? Why else would they need assault weapons? And if that *is* the expectation, then let's be honest—they'd need far more than just those firearms to stand a chance. Should we start stocking weapons of mass destruction at the local convenience store then? Maybe it's time we stop supplying dangerous ideas under the guise of rights.

Indeed, it flies in the face of conventional wisdom in the post-reality world but how is this suggestion less ridiculous than the easy availability of assault weapons? I wish I was not being serious, but in July 2024, a report announced the sale of weapons at vending machines in retail outlets in certain cities of USA, which is beyond dystopian and beyond commentary in the contemporary world.

Of course, there is hand-wringing and heated rhetoric from few sane quarters, but no concrete steps have been taken to address the poor elephant in the room. This has largely normalized extreme violence—the nation accepts it as a cost of modernity, as a bug in the matrix, as a tolerable muddy pebble in the blue waters of the AI era. This is concerning; because what America does today, other countries will follow tomorrow.

And does this attitude which condones the flow of ignorance, encourages incendiary statements and division, and turns a blind eye to the subsequent impact stay confined to a regional, national level?

No.

War and the age of geopolitical conflict: The edge of the abyss

On a global platform, the spread of vicious ignorance, delusion and violence breeds mass unrest, violence and finally war. War, which is startlingly commonplace as I write this in 2023-2024. War, which is diametrically opposite to the unifying goal of the art of knowledge. War, which is woefully contagious and a defining feature of this age of geopolitical conflict.

But surely, these are just idle fears, you say? The educated, the progressive, the intellectual—they will always reject the abhorrent concept of war and choose lasting peace, won't they?

A little backstory before we delve into this:

When I released my first book *Timeless Wisdom for the Modern Age on Bhagavad Gita*, war clouds had begun to gather on the horizon and the aggressive posturing and heated rhetoric were a warning bell for humanity. This was 2021 and the book's prologue laid emphasis on urgent action that was needed to avoid the spectre of war. When I began the second book, the bell was ringing loud and clear. War had broken out between Ukraine and Russia and when I commenced another project, not only was that war continuing, but another one had broken out between Israel and Hamas.

A disclaimer: I don't possess a crystal ball to plan projects. But in an era of multi-polarity, when the war chest is overflowing as is hate speech, when diplomacy is disparaged and global tempers out of control, when the counsel of knowledge is absent, when conflict is considered a boon for business and when division trumps unity, one doesn't need a fancy ball, a psychic or a tarot card to predict the future. The cards are on the table, already.

Now that I'm working on this book, the ringing is a deafening crescendo and there is war all around us.

Sure, anti-war demonstrations by student organizations and peace-loving groups have played out across geographies, but perhaps, their sound waves exist on an unknown frequency that the rest can't connect with. They do not reach their respective leaders who remain nonchalant even as infernos grow larger in different corners of the world.

Which brings us back to the question at the end of the last section—if ignorance may lead to a world war that will be apocalyptic, why not reject it?

Why are dialogue and diplomacy never the answer?

Why are compassion and forgiveness never an option?

Why can we not seek to reconcile instead of retaliating?

Will an eye for an eye not make all blind?

Why are communities not empowered to love but goaded to hate?

Why are weapons of mass destruction created, if not for use?

Why is war accepted as part of human destiny?

Does divine will advocate harm on the blameless?

Can war ever end?

How will it end and, before that, what will it end?

At war: The military-industrial complex at work

Whatever the question, why is the answer always war?

Because its authoritarian proponents do not have to face its furious, fearsome aftermath. The Orwellian state and the military-industrial complex are secure in their palaces and penthouses, away from the blood and the bereavement, the loss and the longing, the destruction and the devastation. No, they are not unaware of the impact of their sorry actions, flashed as they are all over social media and conventional media forms.

They orchestrate war because it is profitable, and allows them to hold on to and grow their stupendous wealth. And they hope that rebranding and repackaging war will make it acceptable, preferable, respectable, and the way things stand, a dominating force of the modern times. Although painted as an altruistic exercise, it is far from it—it is not spurred by a desire to protect the masses or as a fight against injustice, but by a lust for power.

These ignorant blood-soaked choices have brought humanity to a precipice, teetering at the edge with a severe humanitarian crisis affecting millions of civilians in West Asia, Ukraine and parts of Africa. The onslaught of violence they have witnessed on a burning landscape charred by death and displacement, their hearts riven by sorrow, their future overshadowed by loss is inexcusable. Further, climate change has complicated the situation by driving food, water and resource scarcity and creating a fertile ground for new conflicts. The war-inflicted trauma will hurt not just the respective countries, but also the global consciousness. There will be a collective price to be paid, thanks to the god of karma. We may not know when or how, but the bill will come due.

Till then, the deadly brush dipped in the blood of innocents, in the hues of loss, pain and ruin will loom large on our shared conscience. Remember how hard Lady Macbeth tried to wash off the blood from her hands but was unsuccessful? Perhaps we're all in the same boat—scrubbing and rubbing until kingdom come—yet the splatter of blood and the stench of hatred will continue to linger.

You vs the other and you vs the world: The concept of othership

War is a convincing example of how tenacious the pebble of ignorance is and how far it can the push the collective or individual intellect away from rational behaviour. It is not an authentic expression of existence, identity or truth; on the contrary, it is symbolic of the widening chasm between the warring individual and wisdom.

With its proximity to the marshlands of hate, ego and greed, it is the defiant creator of the unsettling concept of the 'other'—the one who is the unfortunate recipient of collective aggressive energies of the larger group. In a social and political setting, this is a community, tribe, religion or sect which appears different, and hence is deemed dangerous.

It is an agonizing process of dehumanizing and debasing another individual/group, which tragically dehumanizes the self. Since the 'other' is considered sub-human, this process extracts a disturbing toll from society, engendering no compassion or mercy, normally reserved for accepted groups or sects. It divides the communities into two groups: us and them.

Even a child knows this is not the way forward, for they are not corrupted by divisive ignorance. But alas, ignorance compels even the so-called evolved modern men, armed with their self-professed infinite wisdom, to draw chalk lines of division, to label those on the other side as 'the other.' And once this is established, they do not hesitate to declare open season for violence.

It is a stark reminder of a checkered past which should have remained in history books but continues to stubbornly surge into the present, proving humanity's worst instincts are alive and kicking.

The anatomy of war

We have to ask ourselves, who really benefits when the voice of truth is silenced, when the concept of othership flourishes and when division is unleashed? Why can we not comprehend the anatomy of war and the process of othering? Why is it everywhere—in hearts, in eyes, in minds, and naturally then, in lives?

The enemy of mankind
Since time most eternal.
The bastion of man's follies
The worst of his instincts
It is war. One of many.

But sooner rather than later
It will draw to an end,
And the battle-weary will realize
That it achieved nothing
But death and destruction
Defeat and despair

It crushed the victor and the vanquished
The warrior and the commoner.

Its gruesome horizon littered with
Elderly abandoned parents

Injured, orphaned children
Victimized women and men.
Entire populations displaced,
Bustling cities under siege
Indigenous communities silenced
Wiped off the face of the earth
As if they never existed.

Oh, some did shed a tear?
But for their own martyrs,
Their ailing, injured, broken
Their feeble, struggling ones.

The compassion reserved for 'your' side.
The cascade dedicated for 'your' people
But it was you who
Defeated them and lost.
Your ego and theirs.
Ours.

Which engendered hate and greed
Which created the other

Which created the battle
With no end, no soul
No respite, no dawn.
No meaning, no purpose.

A struggle with nothing to return from
Nothing to win, and everything to lose.

In this fight over mine and yours
We lost sight of the now

Of the whys and the hows,
Of what was ours and theirs
All of it and none of it.
Maybe some of it?
Maybe none of it.

We lost sight of peace and justice
Of truth and wisdom
Of reconciliation and remembrance
Of knowledge, pure and pristine.

That road would have been rigorous
But a worthy, honourable one
Not unjust, not unkind.
Not blood-soaked, not tear-stained.

It would have been ours to embrace
Ours to build together,
Ours to flourish on, ours to win on,
Like each war is ours to lose.

Rejecting the shape-shifting enemies: Ignorance, division, war

With the shape-shifting enemy ignorance entrenched firmly in the political landscape as well as in minds, we should not be surprised to witness the theatre of war play out across the world. Or that it has the potential to widen but that is a scenario which must be avoided at any cost. There is a reason why statesmen, rationalists and philosophers do not refer to the next big war as the

Third World War but as the last one, for developed nations possesses huge reservoirs of weapons of mass destruction, including nuclear, chemical and bio-weapons which are enough to end civilization as we know it. Enough to turn our Stone Age ancestors over in their graves. This is not what they struggled for over thousands of years, to end up with an uncertain present ravaged by worry and war and a future reeking of instability and intolerance of the other, be it a country, ethnicity, skin colour and viewpoint. Is this progression or regression? What answer will we give to our children if they pose this question to us? Will they applaud us when their heritage is burned to cinder and razed to the ground?

We cannot allow the unpalatable doctrine of war to destroy what our ancestors—scientists, artists and statesmen built over centuries of evolution. It is worth fighting for, it is worth preserving and saving. In the words of Anne Frank, 'I don't think of all the misery, but of the beauty that remains.'

We must ponder over it. War is no longer an unfathomable or ignorable phenomenon occurring in a remote corner of the planet. Because of the deeply connected nature of the economies today, the instability war generates in one country can and does reach the shores of other nations. And it is common knowledge that recurring tidal waves of instability and division can cause irreversible, lasting damage. It may be too late to avoid the current wars, but newer ones can still be prevented and current ones resolved.

If we turn a blind eye to the destruction of the other, be it another country or community, it won't be long before that tsunami will reach our doorstep. Its waves will not discriminate, and sweep up an increasing number of innocents. We cannot stop a tsunami in its tracks but we can reach high ground before it hits. That is, we can prevent the normalization of war, violence, hate speech and ignorance—an illogical, ill-fated use of time, effort, resource.

Otherwise, they will grow like an insatiable black hole, a mysterious cosmic object which devours stars and planets which drop by its neighbourhood. Not to worry, this is not a horror tale. When a radiant star or planet lurks in the vicinity of a hungry black hole, its monstrous power drags the unsuspecting celestial object towards it and in the process, destroys it. It's gravity at work, nothing sinister.

But the sorry mindset which promotes fealty to war is.

Author and pacifist Leo Tolstoy indicted it with his powerful words, 'War is so unjust and ugly that all who wage it must try to stifle the voice of conscience within themselves.'

Paying heed to that powerful voice has never been more needed than the present.

What about the struggle for democracy and human rights, you may wonder?

Yes, we have to fight for justice, but with awareness, meaning and compassion. Standing up for justice should not be considered as noble, logical, yogic or wise, but necessary.

The art of knowledge: A prescription for troubled times, minds

What is also obvious is that just as a disease requires a specific line of treatment, so do modern challenges. For instance, a lifestyle disease requires a lifestyle change to heal- hence the name. Similarly, the scores of challenges created by the gift of materialism, namely ignorance, division, gendered violence, othership and so on also need a cure to address them.

When we do not ignore elementary health issues, why ignore the grave intellectual ones?

What are the apparent causes of strife?

They may vary from country to country but some of them are historical, political or territorial reasons, religious, economic or ethnic conflict, poor leadership, immeasurable arsenal of weapons, propensity to use violence, restive minds, communities divided and lack of authentic information sources. There may be other indicators which hint at future problems including the absence of educational opportunities, abject poverty, unemployment, growing instability, spiraling cost of living hastened by a sense of purposelessness and an absence of human rights and democratic principles.

A quick geopolitical check reveals that the embattled nations facing an inflammatory climate also grapple with food and water insecurity, crippled economies, shattered dreams, eroded identities, and a lack of fundamental freedoms.

How will they focus on meaningful creation, joy, value or prosperity? How will they break the cycle of division and strife if they are perennially distracted by catastrophic levels of ignorance? If they have the propensity to slide into anarchy and chaos, how will they focus on the macro challenges posed by economic, political and cultural uncertainty and climate change amongst others and on individual goals at a micro level?

The rise of Gyan Yoga: A timeless aura. A new era

The soulful teachings of the art of knowledge offer answers to such existential questions along with a roadmap and relevant ammunition to navigate the challenges posed by the fragmented, post pandemic, post-truth digital world. They explore the timeless heritage of ancient Indian philosophy hitherto shrouded in memory and mystery, through the lens of spirituality and science, history and culture. They are not a collection of abstract quotes or garbled mantras insignificant, irrelevant to the minutiae of modern life, but a rational, practical recipe of sustenance, solace and success. They offer:

- A compelling new vision for an era of peace, prosperity and progress.
- An evolved outlook serving as a guiding light for the individual and the community.
- A rational thought process backed by logic which promotes authenticity, acceptance and abundance.
- Clarity and strength to accept and preserve the collective identity.

- Self-knowledge to navigate existential worries.
- Rejection of the materialism driven conditioning which engenders a transactional, parochial and divisive outlook.
- Harmony and balance, and rejection of the grim blindfold of division and distrust.

In a deeply conflicted and divided world, wherein the masses search through and struggle with the rubble of their lives, the tenets of Gyan Yoga arrive as a lush spring of wisdom. With the spiritual lifeline offered by them, they seek to, heal them from the ills of despair, division and discord and to banish the shroud of ego to the footnotes of history. The key tenets are:

- Tenet 1: The Universal Nature and Unity of the Creation Principle
- Tenet 2: The Authenticity Principle
- Tenet 3: The Acceptance Principle
- Tenet 4: The Consciousness Principle
- Tenet 5: The Divinity Principle
- Tenet 6: The *Aham Brahmasmi* Principle

PART B

[illegible] which will be pinned on others. They will over indulge in pleasure, be it food, drink or work and remain utterly careless about the needs or aspirations of others.

A habit of self-analysis of one's own behaviour, motivation, desires and their sources can throw light as to what, why, how and where one is going wrong and ensure corrective measures be implemented for a life of authenticity and purpose.

At the workplace– Impact of Authenticity

Let's see how this plays out in the contemporary workplace, with an example:

Example: Salespersons A and B

Scenario 1: An organization employs Salesperson A who is well dressed, communicates clearly and confidently explains the product features, benefits and special offers to the customer.

Scenario 2: The same organization also employs Salesperson B who arrives late to another customer's office, forgets to the product information, is distracted, bored, does not connect with them and does not understand their needs.

Both possess similar educational qualifications. Both are equipped with tools and resources and carry the same [illegible]

ONE

Tenet 1 of Gyan Yoga: The Nature of Universe and Unity of Creation Principle

The first tenet of Gyan Yoga focuses on the stage where the will of life plays out.

The observable universe: The home of space, time and all existence

The observable universe, as it is referred to in modern science, is the home of space-time, living beings and all existence, including the different forms of energy and matter. It can be classified as—

- **The Gross Universe:** This is the visible form of the universe which encompasses rocky planets, gleaming stars, frozen comets, mysterious meteoroids, natural satellites, distant galaxies and so on. They are crafted from the *panchabhootas*—wind, water, ether, fire and earth.
- **The Subtle Universe:** The non-visible or the abstract part of the universe which consists of forms of energy like light, radio waves and x rays,

> which, although unseen, make their presence felt in numerous ways. For instance, gravity is a potent force of attraction between objects of mass. But it has no fixed particle, colour or form; it is accepted as the omnipresent force which keeps cosmic players in orbit around their stars and in their respective galaxies. Although unseen, it can be measured and exists everywhere at once.

Who created the stars, the galaxies and the universe? How and when did the cosmic drama begin? Remember, these questions have been around since the dawn of time. Perhaps, your mind is teeming with these questions or maybe your inquiry revolves around how you can live your best life. Both sets of questions are valid—science answers the first set, while the second will be addressed in the next chapter.

Science places the date of birth of the present universe at 13.8 billion years when it came into existence as an exploding ball of fire. This was named the Big Bang; well, because it was a pretty fiery affair. But not a loud one as space is a vacuum and possesses no atoms or molecules to transport sound waves. However, scientists remain unsure as to what or who caused the Big Bang, why did it occur or who placed the initial ball of fire in space.

What they know to some degree of certainty is that there exist stunning galaxies or universes in the great beyond, but they remain invisible and out of contact and reach. Because those swaths of space are so distant, the cosmic light originating from some of them is yet to reach earthly shores, hence they have no way of confirming or denying their existence.

A theory of quantum physics states that there are multiple multiverses with space expanding endlessly in all directions, while another states there may be infinite parallel universes with all outcomes playing out simultaneously. Physicists also posit that after a handful of hundred trillion years, the cosmos will cease to exist as all celestial formations will run out of fuel. Their cosmic matter will be consumed by ravenous black holes and nothing will remain in the cold, vast expanse of space. But that is a concern for future generations. For now, the corridors of the universe are expanding at an accelerating rate with light crowned as its fastest element. Undoubtedly, nothing can catch up to light; its speed has been measured accurately at 186,000 miles per second. It travels at the same speed in every direction and is known as the speed limit of the universe.

Then what explains singularity—a point of infinite density and gravity, from which nothing escapes, not even light? It lies at the heart of impenetrable black holes, where the known laws of physics collapse and time itself grinds to a halt. Beyond its mind-bending event horizon, no information survives; no one knows what truly unfolds within its dense, dark core.

This brings us to another kind of singularity—one born not of the cosmos, but of the digital age: the technological singularity. A point where technological growth becomes uncontrollable, unpredictable, and potentially irreversible, ushering in a future with devastating consequences for humanity.

Now, enter artificial intelligence (AI). While we struggle to harness and deploy human intelligence, the advent of artificial intelligence seems determined to wreak havoc on its hapless creator. There is little to no information of its real nature or power, but what is clear is that its potential is unlimited, undefined and uncontrolled. Generative AI has made its presence felt in the finance industry and it is expected to increase global gross domestic product (GDP) by 7 per cent or $7 trillion. As per Goldman Sachs Research, it may boost productivity growth by 1.5 per cent over a ten year period globally.

In healthcare, education, defence, the genie is now a reality. AI controlled drones are already participating in battlefields around the planet and AI applications are replacing portions of the workforce in process-oriented jobs. Eminent scientists and leaders of information technology have asked for a halt to its unchecked growth, with good reason. For a global community reeling with a looming recession, prolonged wars and a cost-of-living crisis, it is a development which must be approached cautiously.

In 2024, the International Monetary Fund report predicted it would impact close to 40 per cent of the world's jobs, replacing some, while assisting others. What's deeply concerning is that it is expected to enhance geopolitical inequalities and widen the wage gap between skilled and unskilled workers. Although the report states wealthier countries are better prepared for adoption of AI, steps must be taken to ensure developing nations are not left behind in this race. In India, AI is poised to transform the business landscape and lead to skill development and greater productivity in a number of sectors including agriculture, defence, cyber security and data analysis and processing. Yes, it may usher in untold efficiencies, but at what cost?

One would do well to heed the parable of Icarus—a timeless warning of what awaits when humanity moves forward with blind ambition, unchecked ego, and without the guiding grace of wisdom.

Be it AI, singularities, black holes, the unobservable universe or the cause of creation, presently, there exist more questions than conclusive answers. This is a limitation inherent in the realm of material knowledge, indeed it reveals a part of the picture but not the full canvas of life.

What does the philosophy of Vedanta say about the nature of the universe?

The outlook of Vedanta: A world within a world

The mystical philosophy of Vedanta offers a unique viewpoint to navigate the mysteries of the universe: it states it undergoes a series of natural cycles of creation and destruction.

However, the present cycle is not the first one, and definitely not the last—the irrepressible universe will continue to manifest, end and remanifest in the future. Its starry energy will continue to circulate and is analogous to the one running through beings. It is the same energy, the same cosmos and the same creation, but in different forms, at varying points of space-time.

Take the cosmic journey of the energy of the being. It unfolds in a similar way to that of the universe—an individual begins as a seed or embryo, grows into an adult before they begin to age and wither away, only to remanifest albeit in a different form. The pure energy flowing through this entire process remains constant; it is indestructible and in motion, even as the play of form continues.

Avyaktadini butanivyaktamadhyani Bharata
Avyakta nidhananyeva tatra ka paridevanaa (BG 2:28)

All beings are unmanifest in their beginning, manifest in the middle stage and unmanifest on destruction. 'Where is the cause of lament?' asks the Gita.

This makes for a startling realization—the universe, with its vast constellations of stars, is not so different from us. And no, I don't mean the stars of celluloid, but those that shimmer quietly in the night sky. Like us, they undergo laborious cycles of birth and rebirth although their charismatic supernova explosions, inscrutable wormholes and galactic black holes are far more intriguing than our run-of-the-mill human cycles.

There are other similarities too. The structure of the human brain mirrors the intricate structure of the cosmos. The incredible placement of thousands of nerves in the brain mirrors the fascinating distribution of the star-studded galaxies; it appears as if the 69 billion neurons in the brain and billions of glittering galaxies in the observable universe are locked in an abiding embrace, scattered over millions of light years but symbiotically connected by an unseen, unknown force.

And that's not all.

The unified nature of the universe: The expression and the expansion

The connection between the universe, the being and existence is expressed in more ways than can be counted, with the truth of mathematics, nature and of life embedded within the elements.

Take the example of the Fibonacci series. For the non-math fans, it is a sequence where each number is the sum of the previous two. It begins with 0, 1 and goes to 2, 3, 5, 8, 13, 21 and so on. Nature uses this interesting sequence to split the tree trunk into two branches, one of those branches splits into two and so on. Similarly, the dewy petals of a flower speak the language of math, and bloom using Fibonacci. Even leaves sprout in this way but unless the veil of ignorance is discarded, the deep linkages between the cosmic elements will never be evident.

This is not confined to flora alone. The Fibonacci spiral is also deployed by arty humpback whales to create bubble traps while hunting in the depths of the ocean. Does that not spell intelligence in nature? It also symbolizes harmony, beauty and order, where each unit is in lockstep with itself and others. Much like the creative cells in the human body discussed in Chapter 1.

Yes, the astounding multiverse is the creative playground for cosmic intelligence which is expressed in the infinite connections between the stars, galaxies, branches, leaves, birds, animals, supernovas and humanity.

In ancient Indian philosophy, this is referred to as the Unity of Creation wherein the beings, the universe and nature are expressed as one complete unit. They may appear dissimilar but their central oneness is unarguably established and illuminated by the synchronised rhythm of existence.

Why is this relevant to contemporary life, to the modern individual?

Amidst the rising waves of division, bigotry and polarization, the Unity of Creation principle offers a sturdy source of stability and renewal. Although it comes from the distant past, it is culturally, intellectually and morally relevant to the age of artificial intelligence with its bold vision of peace and unity. By illuminating the inherent equality of all beings, it presents an evolved vision of harmony and prosperity—where respect, growth, and compassion arise naturally.

The Gita explains:

Atmaupapyena Sarvatra samam pashyati yorjuna
Sukham va yadi va dukham sa yogi parmo mata (BG 6:32)

A yogi seeker witnesses the true equality of beings and cares for their joy/sorrow.

Explaining this concept further, Swami Vivekananda said, 'Knowledge is nothing but finding unity in diversity. Existence without knowledge and love cannot be, knowledge without love and love without knowledge cannot be, what we want is the harmony of existence, knowledge and bliss infinite. That is our goal.'Indeed, one who does not accept this unity with wonder and humility, will achieve little in spite of the dogged pursuit of knowledge.

Mirabai, a leading voice of the grassroots-driven Bhakti movement also laid stress on unity with love and compassion, 'Don't forget love. It will bring all the madness you need to unfurl yourself across the universe.'

In Islam, this is elaborated upon with the concept of *tawhid* or oneness which is belief in the undivided nature of God. A German study by the University of Mannheim studied the correlation between the two and discovered a positive effect of oneness on contentment and balance in life, even while controlling for religious beliefs.

This offers food for thought: across religions and regions, oneness has been stressed upon as the path to a happier, healthier life. Why? To ensure acceptance of the entire universe and its creations, while rejecting the contours of othership and the architecture of division.

Thus, adopting the refined thought process of the Unity of Creation will lead to an enhanced quality of life and an elevated outlook of equity and unity for modern communities.

United by compassion. Disconnected by othership/ marginalization

What is the outcome of abandoning the Unity of Creation principle?

If intellectualism is pursued and practised without compassion and a moral compass, it has the potential to devolve into an ego-laden exercise, or an all-consuming power grab. Under the garb of superiority, (in the absence of equity and diversity), it will always ensure a handful of already celebrated, elevated intellectuals gain access to further privileges and opportunities.

The others will be shut out by the controllers of capital and labour, and will not receive dignity and value for their labour, their prospects crushed by inequality. Is it not a fact today that monopolistic businesses and a handful of economies exclusively enjoy the fruits of civilizational growth while lording over the others, fuelling ever-increasing class, caste and hierarchical divisions?

That is not the path of true growth or to harness the immense benefits of our interconnected existence. Respect and progress belong to every stratum, regardless of caste, creed, religion, ethnicity, or economic status. When every thread, thought and truth is inter-connected, how can opportunity and growth be decoupled?

When the riveting universe is an extension of the very self and community, how can a significant population be condemned to the darkness of division? How will they access peaceful, equitable growth in the face of such headwinds?

As Helen Keller said, 'Science may have found a cure for most evils but it has found no remedy for the worst of them all—the apathy of human beings.'

Saint Tulsidas words are on similar line, 'It is sinful to see the face of a man who does not feel his friend's pain. Treat your own mountain-like pain as though it were a speck. Treat your friend's speck-like pain as though it were a mountain.'

The path of progress and knowledge cannot welcome certain seekers while rejecting others; it welcomes all equally whether a businessperson, artist, lay person, sportsperson, activist, homemaker, me and you. Anyone who possesses the will to seek it, the determination to embark on it, the humility to imbibe it and the passion to pursue it can choose to walk down this hallowed road. All it requires is an intellectual approach to life driven by purpose, persuaded by wisdom and executed by patience.

Imbibing the outlook: A marathon integration of the self, group and universe

With the liberating art of Gyan Yoga, one can go beyond the edges of the universe, beyond the gates of immortality and beyond the rivers of time to forge a future of inclusivity, diversity and excellence; or one can choose to be trapped within the swirls of othership, with a false dawn of unsustainable, lopsided growth.

How can this be prevented and the change be effected?

Enhancing the outlook towards the other, the marginalised and even the self is a long, drawn-out process and can be compared to a marathon.

Friends who participate in marathons share that along with the actual run, training for the run is a deeply satisfying aspect of the experience. It starts small; strength and stamina are built incrementally, and with steady, continuous practice, progress is achieved. Think long distance walks or runs, regular gym workouts, diet discipline and early morning meet-ups which nurture a feel-good factor, a sense of discipline and a spirit of community which defines distance running.

Before the marathon begins, their hearts pound and fear washes over them, but they wait for the training to kick in. And when it does, they set off and achieve their goal. Sometimes, I join them for short walk: they don't break a sweat, although I do, especially, when they seek to persuade me to join them for any upcoming marathon (coughs discreetly).

Which brings up the question, what if they had underprepared? They would have struggled and perhaps given up halfway through. It is with practice and mental fortitude that their kilometres became doable.

So, the secret lies in the homework, something most of us disliked at school. But we couldn't get rid of it then and we most certainly should not get rid of it now, because with homework and all its associated prep work, the difficult becomes the doable. And this is valid for any challenge: physical, emotional or intellectual.

How were a handful of medieval explorers able to sail around the world when there were no advanced navigations systems or state-of-the-art ships, while others feared the mysterious seas? They succeeded because they were determined and prepared as best they could—ready to face the challenge while the doubters hesitated. However, attitudes aren't set in stone. Just as effort is needed to train for a marathon, undivided focus is essential to prepare for the race of life. This involves integrating the different layers of the self and refining one's outlook towards the world.

The Gita explains the clouding of one's outlook by rising doubts and chaos is the handiwork of ignorance:

Tasmad agyana sambhutam hatstahm gyanasinatmana
Chitaiva sanshayam yogam atishthotishtha Bharata

(BG 4:42)

The doubts which have arisen in your heart are due to ignorance and should be slashed by the weapon of knowledge. Armed with yoga, O Bharata, get up and fight.

Fight against what? The ignorance and the uncertainty holding one back.

Nothing objectionable if you do not want to run a marathon but if there is an integrative goal or mindset shift you want to achieve, struggling against ignorance is crucial.

An update: My friends did convince me to participate in the 5 km run and to my surprise, it turned out to be a fun experience, only if your definition of fun includes dragging your half-awake, sweat-inundated bemused self over thousands of metres with half the city gawking at you!

In any case, hardships, races, exams and challenges of the era of artificial intelligence will continue to increase in frequency/size or will appear to snowball; our response has to be calibrated to match their magnitude. So the preparation has to ongoing, not a one-time effort.

Speaking of snowballing challenges, after the marathon, my friends began planning an arduous Himalayan trek and sought to rope me in; calibrating my reaction to that was not easy.

Bringing Tenet 1 into life: Answering the call of wisdom

The point being, mountain or marathon, they are ours for the taking if we so desire. At every foothill, every bend, every turn, reassert a higher choice:

- « Preparation over procrastination
- « Strength over sorrow
- « Compassion over othering
- « Reconciliation over rubble
- « Transcendence over trepidation
- « Wonder over worry

With the awareness of the inter-connectedness of the universe and the Unity of Creation principle, why not:

- **Choose authentic, non-exploitative growth**
  Growing at the expense of another is not authentic progress. For instance, exploitation through colonization destabilizes and haunts the cultural and emotional fabric of affected individuals/ nations. The social damage, economic ruin, cultural despair and hardship it leaves in the wake are unquantifiable, unimaginable. This mode of progress must be rejected by both the layperson and the genuine seeker of knowledge.

- **Choose to reject greed**
  Since the universe and its players are connected, so is the future. Then, so should the resources be. An astute seeker of Gyan Yoga, must strive to imbibe the Unity of Creation principle and ensure shared opportunities, sustainable growth and inclusivity, so that prosperity flows down to every strata of society.

- **Choose confidence over doubt**
  When a curious seeker is besieged by grey clouds of doubt that threaten to turn golden dreams into dust, they must remember that it is stardust. Forged from the same elements as the glistening stars and undergoing similar cycles, they and the celestial objects are in sync, flowing in the cosmic rhythm, so why lose heart? And just as they don't shine for glory, in the same way, their light must allow the self to shine, while also illuminating a pathway for others.

- **Choose patience over quick-fixes**
  As the universe moves through cycles of manifestation and dissolution without much ado, the seeker of knowledge must accept the universality, truth and logic of natural cycles. In doing so, they must choose patience over instant gratification, stability over a false sense of urgency, unity over division, and equanimity over insecurity. That will help them stay focused, whether while being feted or faulted.

- **Choose dialogue over division**
  The Unity of Creation principle offers the seekers a path and an opportunity to heal divisions. After a

prolonged history of conflict, this will require a novel approach, clear-eyed strategic thinking and intentional behaviour. Diplomacy, dialogue, reconciliation measures and trust-building actions while eschewing damaging rhetoric and divisive actions can go a long way to build peace.

As inter-related, multi-dimensional elements, the universe and all its beings with all their dreams, desires and hopes are intimately, infinitely bound together.

Much can be achieved in the absence of war and in the presence of peace. Yes, long-standing conflicts, perpetual wars, intractable economic challenges and the problems of tomorrow will not be solved instantly, and definitely not with a jaded, ignorant outlook. It will require a fresh effort, a marathon effort, a logical, rational one, but as I learnt, it is not so bad or difficult once you prepare for it. What other alternative do we have?

TWO

Tenet 2 of Gyan Yoga: The Authenticity Principle

From the universe, we move on to a dominant player on its stage—the being who arrives with a bundle of existential questions—who am I? What is my body made of, what is my nature and purpose? Why do I behave the way I do? What draws me and what repulses me? And what will be the consequence of my actions? How can I live my best life? What is the law of karma and what is the nature of karmas?

Gyan Yoga possesses the answers related to the nature of the self, the mind-body senses, their building blocks and the mystery of karmas. It states a human being is a mix of the body and the consciousness. But it has not one, but three types of bodies:

- **The gross body:** It consists of the physical body and its organs. Limited in nature, it perishes upon death and returns to its original state of matter.
- **The subtle body or the *kaaran shareer*:** It consists of the mind, the intellect, the ego and *prana* or energy.

- **Causal body:** The inestimable source of the mind and the light of consciousness, it is free from the limiting rules of the universe. It holds the sum of the karmas and adopts a new body when the older one perishes and is discussed further in Tenet 4.

Thus, every being has three bodies with which they interact with the world, with the gross and the subtle body referred to as the mind-body sense complex.

With the finite material senses, the mystical individual drives incredible inventions, impressive discoveries, path-breaking ideas, ground-breaking research and inter-galactic exploration. As the infinite self, they transcend the constructs of space-time, fate and mortality, venturing into the sublime vision of eternity.

Thus, the art of knowledge unilaterally answers the first question who am I—

I am not a material being, but a transcendent, spiritual creation, whose body is crafted from the finest elements of the world. My subtle and the gross body are venerable instruments, which allow me to experience the magic of existence across planes, dimensions and space-time.

And what is the purpose of this earth-bound existence?

Well, there are some philosophers and thinkers who are of the opinion that life has no meaning or sense; the body is crafted from earth, water and fire, will exist for a sizable number of years and pass away based on the alignment of the stars. But this is gross injustice to the esoteric concept of life and the vast potential of the self.

The ancient Indian scriptures adopted a distinct stance; they believed life was pulsing with rich meaning every second of the day, every minute of the hour; its every vibration, thread and dimension injected with hope and harmony. The goal of this blessed life was self-realization achieved by fulfilling one's embryonic potential and elevated purpose.

But realization is not a salient goal to begin with and becomes apparent after the accomplishment of basic needs. This is in line with the Needs Pyramid developed by Abraham Maslow, a well-known psychologist who stated that man would progress towards higher needs after meeting his basic ones. In ascending order, they are:

- Physiological needs
- Safety needs
- Love and belonging
- Self-esteem
- Self-realization

Thus, a lofty goal often becomes evident and urgent only after the fulfillment of basic desires. In the process of meeting these basic and higher needs, one may experience the rollercoaster of life and accumulate a vast store of karmas. But what exactly are these elements we gather as we move through the cycle of life? How can one navigate them or avoid their negative impact?

The mystical nature of karmas: Manifesting destiny

The ancient Indian knowledge traditions believed life was a sacred journey imbued with scores of duties and karmas. One's action carried deep within itself a seed of a reaction—a kind deed led to a positive karma and a bad, no-good, horrible one resulted in a negative one. Whether an action was performed or not, both sets of deeds would generate a result.

What is the nature of this result or karma?

This maybe the age of the temporary, but the nature of fiery karmas is not. These results of actions/choices are semi-permanent and do not dissipate with disease or death. Rather, they are believed to travel over thousands of births to deliver the consequences of action and- thus, the collection of opportune or inopportune moments experienced in a lifetime are a result of their fruition.

One is born and reborn based on these entrenched karmas, which are stored not in a divine ledger but within the confines of the body. So, there is no wishing them away, no eluding their wanderlust or escaping the long arm of their particular brand of justice.

Broadly, they are of three types:

- ***Sanchita karma***: These are the accumulated karmas of the past lives which have yet to fructify.
- ***Agami karma***: These are the karmas which bear fruit in the current life.
- ***Prarabdha karma***: This is the karma of the past which will mature in the future

Thus, every being goes through their compelling loop whether they choose to or not. That sounds rather grueling, isn't it? Because they will add up to a not-so-pretty number, over multiple births, over millions of actions.

Is there any way to avoid the impact of all the actions of all the past lives?

One process alone guarantees this—that of Gyan Yoga.

Let us see how.

Destiny on the side of the intellectual

For the *gyani* seeker, sanchita karma is considered to be exhausted because they are advanced on the wisdom horizon. Since the tides of time do not spill onto their present, the impact of a yesterday or a tomorrow has no binding effect on them.

Even in their current birth, they do not accumulate burdensome karmas. This is not because they renounce worldly life or avoid responsibilities. On the contrary, they fully engage with their duties—at home, at work and within the community—but with the attitude of a non-doer and a non-enjoyer. As a neutral observer, they engage without attachment, without a selfish motive and offer the result of their actions to the divine—in this way, they escape the impact of overbearing karmas.

However, prarabdha karmas do play out in their life but since they are equipoised, they are utterly powerless to disturb them. When their body reaches the destination, all the prarabdha stock is accepted as nullified by the fire of wisdom.

To recap:

- Sanchita or the collected are decimated due to gyan

- Agami or the current are avoided due to sagacity
- Prarabdha are exhausted in the present life and not carried forward in the karma ledger

In the Gita, it is explained simply—

Yathaidhamsi samithognir bhasmasaat kuruterjuna
Gyanagni sarvakarmani bhasmasaat kurute tatha
(BG 4:37)

Just as fire turns wood to ash, the fire of knowledge scorches the results or karmas of material activities.

Thus, it is the intellectual seeker who wins their freedom from the agami, sanchita and prarabdha burden, and revels in the pleasure of liberation. Unlike other yogis, all their bodies transcend mortality, matter and mind, embracing the light of eternal life. Unencumbered from karmic burdens, they do not travel to other realms or manifest in other bodies and dissolve into the structure of the cosmos. Finally, they achieve unity with divinity or *moksha*, the supreme goal of humanity.

Prashantam manasam hyenam yoginam sukhamuttamam
Upaiti shantarajsam brahma bhutam akalmasham
(BG 6.27)

The Gita explains that the yogi whose attention is fixed on divinity will attain happiness and brahma *bhuta*—that is, his identity will merge with divinity and he will be freed from past karmic reactions.

This is the exalted liberation sought after and achieved by the most advanced of gyanis.

Karma and the Creator

Ever wondered, how does the Supreme Creator avoid the impact of the karmas since He is also engaged in management of the cosmos?

> *Na mam karmani limpanti, na me karma phala Spriha*
> *Iti mam yo bhajanti Karmabhir na sa bhajdyate* (BG 4:14)

That is, no work affects me, nor do I aspire for fruits of actions. One who understands this exceptional truth will also not be entangled in fruitive reactions.

The Gita elaborates that the Creator although engaged in constant creation, sustenance and destruction of the cosmos does not accrue any karma, as He does not aspire for the result of His actions.

In this way, the divine and the intellectual avoid the impact of the irksome karmas but what about all others? For the layperson who is not an advanced practitioner of knowledge, does it symbolize they are trapped in a prison of worrisome karmas, doomed to struggle, condemned to an existence without meaning and purpose? Are they powerless beings not in control of their destiny? That sounds rather limiting and upsetting.

Because it is false.

You are in charge of your future and can navigate the impact of the karmic inheritance. Aah, what if you believe you possess little power, talent or potential? Maybe your lived experiences have painted a colourless picture of the future and dimmed the fire within? Why blame the karmas when you have never attempted to navigate them?

Gyan Yoga benefits all, irrespective of the baggage of karmas—

Api chedasi papebhya sarvebhya paapkritam
Sarvam gyana plavaneiva vrijinam santarisyasi (BG 4:36)

The Gita clearly states that even a sinner, with the grace of transcendental knowledge, can cross the ocean of misery, that is navigate worldly life with success.

Consider seeds. Don't even the tiniest of them come loaded with potential—but we have to plant them to discover it. Without that, they will be unable to fulfil their potential. Only a planted seed can grow into a tree, laden with fruits, flowers, leaves, branches—one which can survive countless storms, seasons and cycles of nature.

If a miniscule seed can possess a wealth of potential, how is it possible a lay person infused with mystical properties not possess an iota of talent, in not one but three cosmic bodies? It sounds ludicrous, doesn't it? It may differ from person to person but there is no one who is not blessed with unique gifts.

Declining the destiny: Enter the Authenticity Principle

In the ordinary course of things however, we are unable to accept our unlimited potential. We reject the power, suppress the talent, ignore the call of the self or of destiny and remain uncaring about accumulating regrettable karmas. Uninspired and uncreative, we do not seek to comprehend the canvas of bodies, dimensions and planes on which we operate and obsess over insignificant drawbacks, quirks or flaws.

Consider a koel bird. Ever wonder why the dusky bird does not hesitate to sing? Why does it not think twice before taking flight? Why does it not doubt the melody of its voice, or the strength of its wings? It is because it is in its nature to sing; because it is in its nature to fly.

Or consider a curving river—it does not hesitate to cut across wooded green valleys and fertile plains. It flows because it must. Similarly, it is the nature of dark clouds to drift across the pale blue sky, and of the dancing wave to rise and fall. Or take a jaunty peacock. As it dances in the rain, it does not hesitate to stand tall, and reveal itself in all its beauty, unapologetically displaying its striking iridescent blue green feathers. Similarly, a tiger does not roar shyly, nor does the sky stretch half-heartedly across the horizon. All thrive in their wholesomeness, rawness and sheer flawlessness.

Nature is crafted to perfection, and we accept its creations as they are—without question.This is what the logic of the Fibonacci sequence demonstrated in Tenet 1. But we overlook the fact that we are a part of nature-man is nature in motion which makes him immaculate too. Still, we hesitate to accept the exquisite completeness of the self. When birds, animals, trees, mountains and rivers do not hesitate, why should we? They accept themselves with drawbacks and strengths, why can we not?

If we do not have faith in the self, how will we fulfil the raw potential? Understandably, the battle of faith and doubt has been in play since the birth of time but it is one which is winnable. Like the fierce battle between *vidya* or knowledge and avidya, maya or ignorance. Which is perhaps the same old battle. They may appear divergent, there may be wildly different, superficial factors driving them; but if we probe and prod, we will discover ignorance within the beating heart of doubt.

As mentioned in the introduction, the human body is a faultless creation, greater than the sum of its parts. It can empower one to curate a life where they can be their best self, and to skilfully navigate the karmas, the three bodies and their destiny.

As a symbol of excellence in nature, it is one's duty to utilize their flawless symmetry and luminous talent and to fulfil the destiny. Why be trapped in a prison of karmic baggage with knowledge? Why not transcend the pre-determined destiny and flourish with authenticity, abundance and acceptance.

The thought process of Novak Djokovic, one of the finest tennis players of the generation spells out this approach—'I would not change anything in my life. I always did everything the best I knew at the given moment. I made a lot of mistakes but at least I was authentic. Myself. A hundred times I would rather choose to be myself than go along with the system that is popular these days.'

What is this quest for authenticity and the authentic nature of the self, you may wonder?

The Indian seers and sages unequivocally stated the authentic nature of the self was love, duty, excellence, faith, compassion, harmony and joy. This driving factor ensured comfort and peace from the performance of duty, from assuming the responsibility of a loved one, from charity and by helping one pay it forward and so on.

Haven't you read of patrons in cafes purchasing a beverage for the next person in queue? Maybe, they do so to spread positivity or to earn bountiful karmas or maybe it is hardwired in us to do so.

Yes, the act of giving reduces karmic load and Chapter 17 of the Gita elaborates it is a sincere duty to donate and share resources but offers a corollary—

- There should not be an ulterior motive.
- It must be directed towards the needy
- It should be offered at the appropriate place
- And with a pure intention

If a donation is performed with the intention of future gain, it will transform into an investment. Similarly, if it is driven by an ego-laden mind, it will not placate the score-keeping karmas; conversely it may increase their tally.

The law of motion and karma: Science meets philosophy

What if you possess a scientific outlook and do not believe in traditional karmic heritage or in ancient philosophy, spirituality or religion?

No problem. Then, you can accept Newton's Third law of Motion which states that every action will have an equal and opposite reaction. (This is what the law of karma states too, that there will be an equal result of every action.) Whichever path you choose, science and/or philosophy either way, the result will accrue in some form or another.

Since forces work in pairs—the force of integrity will generate a positive energy, similarly, an unethical one will generate a turbulent negative one. Science has shown that energies vibrate at a higher frequency when we form synergies and networks. In essence, we are fields of energy, constantly communicating with other energy fields—be it nature, universe, or fellow beings.

This is what the principle of karma also states: The road to a meaningful life is paved with the sturdy bricks of ethical purpose.

Why not combine the best of science, philosophy, artificial intelligence and spirituality to navigate the ecstasies and excesses of modern life with ease?

Cause and impact of inauthenticity

What causes one to be overcome by inauthenticity, to lose touch with or doubt the self? It may be due to a lack of knowledge or due to the enchanting nature of materialism. They can push one away from knowledge, making life's challenges appear burdensome.

You may want to examine how far or close you are to your authentic identity with a few questions—

Do you feel abnormally stressed and complain you never have any time or energy? Are your desires and wants increasing with the passage of time and when you cannot meet them or if you do meet them, you react with violent anger, greed, lust or denial? Do you live in constant anguish, fear and insecurity? Do you suffer from an inexplicable emptiness or a dearth of joy? Do you possess a scarcity mindset? Do you assume you are superior to the other or a victim of the other? Do you possess feelings of hatred towards a stranger on the basis of social media? Is your life devoid of contentment, gratitude or peace? Do you believe that hurting others is justified? Do you believe in the doctrine of war?

If you answered yes to most of these questions, you are pretty distant from the authentic nature. Although this thought process is accepted and celebrated in society, it is far from ideal. Stress, fear, anxiety, greed and anger are normal emotions and each serve a purpose. But when they proliferate, they create trouble at home, in the workplace, the community, with friends, neighbours and even in the country as a whole.

For instance, these emotions may make their presence felt in the following way in one's personal life—

- One overwhelmed by increased levels of stress will react with ego, anger, lust and greed. They will instigate quarrels at home due to an inflexible, selfish outlook. They will demand respect, but not offer it
- In the workplace, they may demand hard labor from others without putting in comparable effort, or without providing fair compensation to those who do.Their ignorance will lead to failure, the

> fallout of which will be pinned on others. They will over-indulge in pleasure, be it food, drink or work and remain utterly careless about the needs or aspirations of others.

A habit of self-analysis of one's own behaviour, motivation, desires and their impact can throw light as to what, why, how and where one is going wrong and ensure corrective measures are implemented for a life of authenticity and purpose.

At the workplace: Impact of inauthenticity

Let's see how this plays out in the contemporary workplace, with an example.

Example: Salespersons A and B

Scenario 1: An organization employs Salesperson A who is well-dressed, communicates clearly and confidently explains the product features, benefits and special offers to the customer.

Scenario 2: The same organization also employs Salesperson B who arrives late to another customer's office, forgets to cite product information, is distracted/bored, does not connect with them and does not understand their needs.

Both possess similar educational qualifications. Both are equipped with tools and resources and carry the same product. You tell me,who is more likely to close the sale?

It will be Salesperson A, because the prospective customer will trust their recommendation, not the under-confident mumblings of Salesperson B. Salesperson B's lack of knowledge, self-awareness, dwindling enthusiasm and engagement will hinder him from forming a relationship with the customer and from presenting the required solution. Perhaps, he may miss out on sharing product highlights, discounts and benefits, which will further affect the chances of closing a sale.

This is symptomatic of a larger problem. If B is not committed to their duty, and especially if this is part of a pattern, it may indicate a lack of interest in growth, and excellence. If they can shirk professional responsibilities, it suggests they may also neglect personal duties. This will not only hamper personal development but can also impact the organization's bottom line.

In the future, if and when a new product is launched, who will be considered an integral part of the rollout—the salesperson with the finger on the pulse of the customer or the one who speaks in generalities? The one with a proven track record and a penchant for excellence, of course.

In this example, Salesperson B's education did not reflect in their behaviour and remained bookish information, (which was not optimized). Although both possessed the same level of education and offered the same product, A excelled because they implemented the learnings while B languished because they did not.

Can Salesperson B claim they were not aware of the job responsibilities? Maybe but wilful ignorance is not an excuse for failure—it is not a mere mistake but a gross neglect of potential.

The point I'm making is—we may assume a significant level of education is correlated with wisdom but this may not always hold up to scrutiny. Whether it is a salesperson, CEO, vendor or manager, if their performance and outlook is not elevated by their education, it should be considered akin to ignorance. If education does not reflect in the work, in the interactions and in the quality of thought, is it really education in the true sense of the word?

Duty to knowledge, duty to self

At the workplace, it is an unavoidable duty to equip the self with skills and knowledge necessary to perform with excellence and to meet the needs of the customer. Whether work, education, self-growth or life, it is vital to stay ahead of the curve with training/learning opportunities and to implement those learnings with passion. As a manager/leader, this will also include embracing innovation, duties, ethics, responsibilities and moral values, which is the complete role of the knowledgeable leader.

Knowledge also dictates that compassion must not be reserved for others alone but also for the self. As a manager, this means jogging the extra mile and caring for the team, sharing profit/praise, balancing working hours, understanding their aspirations and fostering innovation while taking care of the self. This will signify acceptance of all responsibilities of the role.

But true innovation, good leadership skills, the best pitch, the finest creation- will not occur accidentally. You will have to plan for them and strive to realize them.

What if ignorance plays spoilsport? What if stress rears its ugly head?

If you suffer from uncontrollable stress and fear, it will be a drain on your intellectual, physical and emotional energy. If you believe—I can never perform quality work, I do not have potential, I will never fulfil my ambition and I will perform if and when I become the top manager, you will become a barrier to your own success. It may sound counterintuitive, but you must strive for excellence and self-belief—because it is the only true approach to both work and life. Excellence is not an occasional indulgence; it is an expression of the authentic self. Even in the face of stress or anxiety, you must continue to perform your duties to the best of abilities, and avoid unhealthy indulgences that can weaken the mind.

The Gita adds—

Ya nsiha sarva bhutanam tasyma jaagarti sanyami
Yasyaam Jagrati Bhutani sa Nisha pashyato muneh

(BG 2-69)

What is night for the rest is the time of awakening for the one with a controlled mind and what is the day is the time of sleep for the wise.

Extolling the virtue of vigilance, it encourages the wise to stay cautious of the creeping shadows of temptation.

Those who are inexperienced will allow their guard to drop and expose themselves to incessant desires.

The Gita further clarifies—

> *Nasti budhir ayuktasya na chayuktasya bhavana*
> *Na chabhavayatah asantasya kutah sukham* (BG 2-66)

That is, one who is not rooted in consciousness will not possess a steady mind. They will be devoid of peace and without that, there will be no happiness.

A tryst with authenticity: Immortality ahead

Now that you are aware of Tenet 1 and 2 of Gyan Yoga and perhaps, seek to enhance the quality of your karmas and of your life, what should you do if someone undercuts, cheats or seizes your rightful share of success? What if they remain unbothered about their karmic burden? Should you abandon your principles, too?

Why not question this? Why should we spoil our karmas if others are doing so? Or do you believe they can steal your destiny or the fruit of the karmas—deserving or damning? You should not, it is not possible.

Indeed, what you do not possess, you cannot cede and what you do own, no one can help themselves to. For a brief period, it may appear that someone you consider a competitor has stolen a march over you or usurped your share of the reward, but that is a material illusion. Soon, they will be answerable for their bag of quirky karmas while your priority should remain advancement on personal/professional goals.

Irrespective of the ways of the world, what is yours will stay yours;in any case, you cannot outrun or outgun karmas. Across geographies, across the horizon of time and through uncountable births, they will give chase and hold you and them accountable, which is both alarming and reassuring at the same time.

The Gita advises one to focus on the right *karm* to achieve lasting success and excellence—

Partha naiveha namutra vinashastasya vidyate
Na hi kalyanakrit kashcid durgatim tata gachati
(BG 6:40)

That is, it reassures one engaged in noble activities (right karm) that they will never meet with destruction either in this or the spiritual world.

Inspiration at the summit: Example of the mountain whisperer

The rousing story of the brave mountaineer and explorer Sir Edmund Hilary from New Zealand stands as a testament to the principle of authenticity and the power of self-belief. It offered inspiration to me not because I aspire to be a climber—the entry barrier of sub-zero temperatures is a major deterrent but because of what the feat represented to humanity.

Climbing an unclimbable snowy peak above 8000 metres, that too in exacting conditions, with oxygen in short supply was a tall order. Naturally, this seemingly impossible goal had never been accomplished before.

But it was not a chimera for the resilient mountaineer Hilary and his *sherpa* Tenzing Norgay who possessed an abundance of will power, resilience and a never-say-die attitude. They faced a hard road and had to stand up to the naysayers of whom there were plenty, and the fear-mongers who were in abundance. However, their purpose dwarfed and dispelled the dark clouds of fear and doubt.

Inclement weather, unnavigable zones and insurmountable problems offered new complications and enhanced existing ones. But failure was not an option and they plodded on to achieve what was once considered to be unattainable. As you may be aware, on the fateful morning of May 29, 1953 they reached the summit of the mighty Everest, being the first in the world to do so. And in the process, they inspired all of us to scale our Everests.

Since then, this feat has been replicated many times over; but it needed bold minds, and pioneering hearts to do it before others could follow suit. A number that has grown exponentially, as shown in a recent viral social media picture: the once unconquerable Mount Everest facing traffic jams, with endless queues of mountaineers patiently snaking around its slopes, waiting for their moment in the sun.

This incredible achievement offers valuable lessons. Firstly, like the illustrious climber, we must continue to scale the mountains on our path; they may not be blanketed in snow, but draped in fear, anger or pride but that should not deter us. Secondly, we must nurture courage; this will motivate the self and others. Thirdly, being the first mover has its advantages but that should not be the driving factor/constraint. As long as the purpose is authentic, we can continue down the treacherous trail of our choice, or up the frosty slope in this case.

Finally, we should not allow others to define who we are, what we can or cannot achieve. Sir Hilary was a mountaineer who was aware of the depth of his potential—it allowed him to attempt an expedition considered impossible in those times and to persevere even when the mountain turned hostile.

This is applicable to all of us. If you are a painter, dancer, business person, traveller, manager or employee with an unattainable goal you can adopt the mindset of an unstoppable mountaineer—advancing as the embodiment of authenticity, and as a force within the cosmos that seeks change, drives clarity, and builds conviction..

Yes, it will not be a cakewalk. On this path, there will be no defined trails; you will have to build them yourself. Because only you know your destination and capability, so you will have to realize them by the dint of your effort. If your vision is broad and purpose pristine, you will succeed. Why pay heed to those who won't believe in you? It is enough if you and your family and/or friends do.

I know it sounds unreal, and you may believe it sounds good only in books, but you have to answer the call of destiny. Till you don't, till you avoid the authentic nature, the searing truth, your truth, the struggle will continue, growth will be limited and stagnation may occur, because life will bring you back again and again to the same place, till it is answered.

Fear vs Faith: A personal example will highlight this

My story is not of a chilly mountain I scaled, but one of doubt and fear. After the book on the art of action, the next subject on the horizon was the art of knowledge, but I was hesitant to initiate research. For months, I dillied and dallied, should I begin, could I begin? Could I do justice to it? It is the domain of intellectuals, icons and enlightened souls and the lives of Buddha, Swami Vivekananada, Mahatma Gandhi and other leaders who serve as an inspiration to the world. Their voices represent the finest expression of humanity, symbolizing the confluence of dharma, divinity and wisdom. And continue to unite hearts and minds through the realization of the amaranthine truth.

So you can see why it appeared daunting? A few months passed but I never stopped mulling over it. Then, something happened which shifted the needle.

One fine day in August 2023, my husband announced that we had secured the tickets for a pilgrimage to Tirupati. We had been planning for 7-8 months so this was a lucky break. After the pandemic receded in January 2023, we had attempted to seek *darshan* with extended family, but upon reaching Tirumala discovered it was an unusually busy day there. Every day, the revered land sees millions of devotees pouring in at all hours, but that day was exceptionally busy. We discovered it would take about 7-8 hours to receive the blessed darshan, and were ready to wait. It was a pleasant morning, our mood was upbeat and the crisp air infused us with fragrant hope.

Unfortunately, as the sun rose over the horizon, a relative fell ill, and we were faced with the difficult decision of turning back. It was disheartening first—to have set out on a pilgrimage only to return empty-handed, so to speak. Yet, I did not allow it to demotivate me.

If it had occurred a few years ago, I would have fretted and fumed. But my exploration of the art of devotion and the art of knowledge had stood me in good stead. It removed misconceptions which can complicate the relationship with the divine, the most natural one in the world.

Often, fear and doubt instill negativity and lead to an abundance of superstition and delusion, not the best mix for any relationship. Thankfully, the tenets inspired me to not overthink run-of-the-mill events and not fall prey to conjecture and doubt.

Only the most fortunate devotees receive a glimpse of Lord Balaji, when He wills it. I safely concluded it was a simple case of timing mismatch, not an indication of deep divine displeasure. The travel to the blessed land was an opportunity for spiritual connection, not a commercial one. And when I was ready to accept the reward(the proposed darshan), I would have to accept the flip side(the non-darshan) and that too as a gift, without considering it an ill-omen. I reasoned with the self: if I could not receive blessings in Tirumala, I could receive them at home post the morning prayer, because isn't He everywhere and could He not bless from His divine abode?

This motivated us to keep the faith and months later, on 21 August 2023, we secured the tickets again and were blessed with the sacred darshan of Lord Balaji. What unfolded next demonstrated that divine generosity truly knows no bounds.

Within a month of the first darshan, in a serendipitous turn of events, I received another one at the sacred Tirupati temple in Chennai. I have been a resident of the city for a significant portion of my life but this was my maiden visit, a surprising oversight. I may have missed one darshan, but received two in a matter of months. This is why the saying 'there may be delay, but no darkness in the sacred realm' contains more than a grain of the cosmic truth. For when the divine blesses, he does so with ample abundance.

That evening, instead of heading out for a customary walk, I switched on the laptop and typed out the words 'the art of knowledge' on Microsoft word. I don't prefer to write in the evening and had not planned to begin any time soon. But to my surprise, the words flowed. Perhaps it had no connection to the blessed darshans—or perhaps it did. All I know is that it moved me to finally attempt a subject close to my heart, one I had been actively avoiding. And for me, that was enough.

I decided to approach it with the humble outlook of a student on a quest, of a curious explorer on a voyage of growth, while inviting like-minded explorers to join in. It was challenging, much like scaling an 8,000-metre-plus mountain. But when the brave mountaineers didn't stop, how could I?

Sometimes, many times I did attempt to hold myself back due to fear and doubt but it is not the best approach to writing or towards anything else for that matter. At least, I didn't quit and allowed the subject to lead me. Which brings me to another learning nestled within the experience—It is natural to possess self-doubt, lots of it, but it should not result in the abandonment of the goal.

Does the winding river pause when it encounters a sharp bend? Does the gentle breeze tremble when it runs into the dense forest? Does the merry bird halt at the sight of dark clouds? No, they continue to carve out their destinies, proceeding with nary a pause.

Why should we allow the steep mountain, the thick grasslands, the frigid weather, the sharp bend of stress or the bleak forest of abominable doubt to slow us down then? Maybe they are not meant to obstruct, but to challenge and inspire. The ups and downs, the yeses and nos, the valleys and mountains, the oases and the deserts—they will continue to flow. But they are evanescent. And we are not. This isn't about being stubborn; it's about having faith in our authentic vision and potential. Okay, maybe it's also about being a little obstinate too.

As mystical beings, we are constantly evolving, transforming and growing and so is the lush landscape of knowledge. Then, how can the learning process stop, how can growth be put on hold and potential paused? How can inauthenticity or doubt prevent the accomplishment of goals and the march of progress?

Bringing Tenet 2 into life: Fulfilling the authentic potential

When should you begin this quest for knowledge?

Perhaps, you may seek to begin once you are appointed CEO, after joining a start-up, after retirement, post implementing a five-year plan or after unearthing the elusive time to spare, the urban legend which one may have heard of but which no one seems to possess?

Well, why not start as soon as possible?

Can anyone keep the rising sun down? Not as far as science knows, even after the longest of nights, it will rise to wipe away the inky darkness of the past, heralding a new dawn. Just like the sun follows its path, we must follow ours and embrace destiny. Just like ignorance cannot stay under wraps, the stunning light of the being cannot remain in the shadows. So start as soon as possible and as a free, bold, creative, independent mind, make abiding contributions to the family, workplace, community, nation and world.

Along with the Gita, the ancient Upanishads also state the same—the strength and immortality we need must be derived from the self. Because real strength is self-awareness and knowledge. It can bestow eternal life and infinite success. Here, immortality does not refer to the years one will walk the earth but undeniable power and unremitting excellence which confers unassailable intellectual strength and indestructibility

Otherwise, you may be left with a bunch of regrets or with the awareness that you did not do the best to achieve the potential. Do you want to end up imagining what you could have achieved if you had not stopped yourself from chasing after a goal?

Fear of criticism, failure or self-doubt may prevent you from following the dreams or expressing the needs of the authentic self. For instance, after a certain age, you may hesitate to put on your dancing shoes or learn a new skill because of what 'society may say'. A young man may hesitate to polish his culinary skills because it is (still) considered to be a woman's responsibility. Or a woman may hesitate to apply to the armed forces because she is expected to join the family business. A child may hesitate to share his dreams of travel and a graduate may hesitate to share his fears of the future. But lazy stereotypes serve none, harm the fragile, instil shame and fear.

If you are tired of holding yourself back, exhausted that it is making you sick, express yourself in a manner which makes you feel seen, heard and understood. Bottling the self will foster grief and drive you towards despair. Only a life where you can be the authentic self will heal, satisfy and fuel you—with a purpose, a direction and a future created in line with the dreams. There is one you, so the track has to be customized for you, by you.

You owe it to yourself—

- To live the life's purpose
- To achieve goals
- To express creative needs
- To accept strengths and weaknesses
- To engage with an abundance of joy
- To flourish with self-respect
- To live with the truth, aligned to ethical values.

In her book *Becoming*, Michelle Obama, the former First Lady of the United States, explained this succinctly, 'It's not about being perfect. It's not about where you get yourself in the end. There's power in allowing yourself to be known and heard, in owning your unique story, in using your authentic voice.'

Thus, it is a solemn duty to use your unique gifts and voice for the purpose they were granted. You may feel a goal has already been accomplished—why write a book, sing a song, start a business, or explore a project when others have done it before? But they haven't been accomplished by *you*. They need *your* voice, *your* vision, and *your* unique perspective. Just like the koel's call, your voice is meant to be heard.

You cannot avoid the authentic self any more than you can avoid your shadow. It will accompany you no matter where you go, whether you like it or not, whether you want it to or not.

Yes, not all of us can be artists, singers, dancers or sportspeople, not all of us may get the opportunity to follow our passion as an occupation, but if we invest even a little effort in nurturing all aspects of the self, it will offer great rewards.

If you approach any act or life itself with authenticity and the placid spirit of yoga, it will be elevated to the level of excellence. Art, dance, travel, poetry, gardening, cooking, science or business, they can offer a deep sense of satisfaction, purpose and meaning along with a valuable outlet of creativity and self-expression. This can be extended to the goal as well.

Who says work or duty cannot be creative, nourishing or joyful?

Avoiding the duty or the purpose, avoiding creativity and innovation, suppressing the natural flow of the self is against nature because it is inauthentic. It is natural—

- To celebrate and nurture creativity, to examine the same in innovative ways and to come up with myriad alternatives.
- To navigate the imposing karmas and to go beyond their horizon.
- To flow uninterrupted in spite of barriers put in different bullet as a point.
- To follow the larger vision with fearless grace
- To tap the boundless spring of innovation
- To seek progress for all

If we were not hardwired for authenticity, creativity, excellence and boldness, we would not have continued to evolve or survive for so long.

We should not need an advanced form of yoga to tell us that '*The privilege of a lifetime is to become who you truly are.*'— Carl Jung, founder of analytical psychology.

THREE

Tenet 3 of Gyan Yoga: The Acceptance Principle

Tenet 2 of Gyan Yoga, the Authenticity Principle leads into Tenet 3, the Acceptance Principle. But acceptance of what?

Ancient cultures describe statesmen, leaders, saints, mystics and yogis, who after imbibing wisdom, were first to accept how little they knew. Certainly, the nature of wisdom is immeasurable, infinite and the ancient philosophers exploring its origin/mysteries realized as much.

Greek philosopher Socrates believed, 'The only true wisdom is in knowing you know nothing.' On similar lines, Chinese philosopher Confucius reflected—'Real knowledge is to know the extent of one's ignorance.' The French writer and philosopher Voltaire agreed, 'The more I read, the more I acquire, the more certain I am that I know nothing.'

Separated by years and borders, German scientist Albert Einstein arrived at a similar conclusion, 'The more I learn, the more I realize how much I don't know.'

Herein lies the paradox at the heart of this liberating

journey—the more one learns, the more they realize how vast the scope of knowledge is and how limited the faculties of the mind are. The wisest are the first to admit they know the least; this is why they are never arrogant and those who are arrogant are not considered wise.

The wise humbly accept the limited nature of their knowledge quotient and embark on a life-long, albeit, a non-linear affair to imbibe its esoteric essence. Their goal is not the mere acquisition of facts and statistics, which can devolve into an exercise to placate the ego. In the words of Greek philosopher Plato, 'The highest form of knowledge is empathy for it requires us to suspend our egos and live in another's world.'

Thus, the goal of the journey of knowledge, of the intellectuals and the seekers on this path and indeed of the Acceptance Principle is to accept life with all its complexities and strive for not only personal but collective growth and liberation.

But what prevents this from materializing? The sweeping powers of the ego.

A shloka from the Upanishads elaborates:

Twam stree tvaw pumanasi
Tvwam kumara uta va kumari
Tvam jirna dandena vanasi
Tvam jata bhavasi vishwatamukhah
(Shwetaswatara Upanishad)

You are the woman, you are the man, you are the youth and the maiden, you are the one who suffers in old age, and you are the one whose faces are turned in all directions. That is, whether man or a woman, old or young, happy or sad—they are various facets of humanity undergoing the natural cycle of evolution. These ever-changing forms add complexity to the play of life, but need to be accepted at all stages. What purpose will non-acceptance serve? But this is easier said than done.

In the next chapter, Tenet 4 of Gyan Yoga will elaborate on the eternal nature of the Consciousness Principle. So who or what is it navigating the above-mentioned winds of change? The body.

Instead of wearing the seasons of nature and the emotions of life with equipoise, it struggles against them. This is the work of malicious ego, not of knowledge. Along with generating instability, the false ego invents the labels of division and strife and engenders a non-accepting attitude, be it towards change or the perceived other.

For example, one with wealth may look down upon the marginalized. One from a first world nation may look down upon the developing world.

If you are brawny, you may believe you will remain so forever, Gen X may believe they will remain youthful always, while the privileged may believe the good times will stay loyal throughout their lives. Although the tenets of the Art of Knowledge are not ambivalent on the equality of beings, but while interacting with the external world, who remembers tenets and teachings?

But it is a matter of destiny playing catch-up. What will also catch up is age which is but a reflection of you, in the future. This is what the Upanishads attempted to convey in the shloka above.

Ageing is a part of existence like birth, evolution, profit or loss although we fervently hope we won't have to accept it but dismayingly, these stages will arrive without a knock.

However, change is an incontrovertible truth; rejection will not stall the inevitable. The march of time will stop for none—hair will whiten, wealth may depart, autumn may set in, but the spring in the step and the twinkle in the eye must remain.

Is this possible? How can we navigate the changing nature of the world, of the self, and of the others, of the flow of emotions and fortune? How can we practise the ever-wise Acceptance Principle in real-time? How can we accept the vastness of the knowledge factor with our basic material faculties?

The best of Japanese wisdom: The past for the future

You may have heard of Wabi Sabi, an ancient Japanese concept which champions acceptance of the impermanent, changing nature of the cosmos. Derived from the lofty tenets of Buddhism, it celebrates life and nature in all their rugged glory complete with flaws, foibles, faults and failings.

Further, their ancient art form of Kintsugi or broken pottery offers a metaphor for life; it considers the broken more aesthetically pleasing compared to the original. It elaborates that with the passage of time, objects may lose shape, their glow may fade and their beauty may dim. Still, they must be accepted as alluring, chipped corners and cracks notwithstanding.

Not merely accepted, but joyfully celebrated. This is an acknowledgement and celebration of the fluid nature of existence.

This is also the insightful message of the Acceptance Principle to accept change if you seek to better navigate the chaos and complications of life. Then if and when a misadventure chips away at the self-worth, when life drags away youth or when karma pays a visit to settle scores, you will be able to treat the self not as damaged goods but as an aesthetic piece of art or pottery as the case maybe.

What happens in the usual course of events?

We refuse to accept the wounds, scars, stages and seasons of life and misunderstand the nature of the self, the other, the world. Disoriented, disconnected and dejected, we avoid performing the role and duty in the workplace, community, country. Confounded by the connection to each other, the cosmos and the sloping mountains, lush forests, healing sunshine, powder blue sky, raging rivers, fertile soil, whispering wind and the fathomless ocean, we treat the self as an entity functioning in isolation.

What are the consequences of non-acceptance of the self/events and the connection with nature?

The Acceptance Principle: A vision of integration

The Acceptance Principle issues a rallying cry as well as a prophetic warning—rejection of reality or the lived experience will cause an acute sense of dejection, sorrow, anxiety, stress and anger.

How should one react to difficult times?

Yahasarvatranabhisnehas tat tat prapya subhasubham
Nabhinandati na dweshti tasya pagya pratishtitha

(BG 2-57)

The Gita says that one should be unaffected by the fortunate or the unfortunate turn of events. When one neither hates nor praises what they receive, they are said to possess true knowledge.

Here, unaffected refers to the quiet acceptance of change as a seasonal, cyclical occurrence with a non-permanent, non-binding nature. Thus, it inspires the seeker to stay stable in the face of difficulties.

The is further explained by Saint Kabir:

Kabira khada bazar mani, mangen sabki khair
Na kahu se dosti, na kahu se bair

A mystic in a market, a stand-in for the material world, must bear no ill will, neither be overly attached to another. Crucially, they must maintain the equilibrium amidst the flow of commerce or culture and accept the torments and triumphs as a part and parcel of existence.

This requires two discriminatory powers:

- **Separating the right from the wrong:** For the first stage, one must be able to pick and choose the elevated action from the bevy of wrong ones.
- **Truth and false:** In the next stage, one must be able to distinguish between the shades of reality and perception. This is further discussed in Tenets 4, 5 and 6.

Logic of the Acceptance Principle: Masterful yet effortless

Thus, the evolved logic of the Acceptance Principle inspires us to trust the process and nature of the universe—to accept whatever it sends our way be it praise or blame, win or loss, yes or no, with equanimity and humility. We will meet both, might as well befriend them. There is no one who will not face the dual sides of the coin—you will be no exception and neither will I be.

The more you accept, the better you will flow with the gentle cosmic rhythm. With an equable attitude towards the swirling clouds of change, you will be able to witness and accept the rich wisdom ingrained in the quiet unfolding of the universe. Indeed, there exists a rational reason behind every action, every no and perhaps every mountain/marathon/monster, although it may not be evident.

Even though it may be painful to accept a tough situation in the moment, it must be faced with the same determination as the alternative. Acceptance does not signify capitulation—it is a rich opportunity to analyze, adjust and restart with renewed energy, reassessed goals and a refreshed approach.

What purpose will rejection of, say, the Covid-19 pandemic, which unleashed itself on the world from early 2020 onward would have served? Or take Iceland. In early 2024 in Iceland, a fiery volcano exploded thrice in a month after being dormant for years. The Icelanders were forced to accept this. When all their lives they had nestled amidst its pristine beauty, they could not reject its catastrophic fury.

In the future, what they can do is prepare for such an eventuality and ensure contingency measures are in place to protect the residents.

In the Gita, this intuitive acceptance requires a trait known as courage of mind or *titiksha*—acting consciously where action is needed, accepting what cannot be changed and avoiding thoughtless reaction/response.

Matrasparshastu Kaunteya sitosna sukha dukhada
Aagamapaayino nityastams titiksshasva Bharata

(BG 2:14)

That is, joy and sorrow are cyclical like the seasons of summer and winter: you must be able to tolerate them with titiksha.

With titiksha, you can navigate change with power and poise. Remember, you are the Authenticity Principle as per Tenet 2—you don't need anyone to save you; you can save yourself. Is that not hugely freeing? That you do not need a rescue mission from the world, one which is barely able to sustain itself? With faith, accept the self as your superhero. Luckily, no mask is needed for this adventure.

What is imperative, however, is knowledge—to create and collaborate, to grow and innovate, and to forge ahead with fresh thinking and intentional effort.

Benefits of the Acceptance Principle: Strategic, spiritual

The Acceptance Principle will empower you to view life with its black and white moments, cloudy and sunny days as a precious, perfect gift.

- It will nurture critical thought to reject the propaganda and the damaging narrative imposed by the pebbles of ignorance.
- It will offer pure freedom from the agony of the human condition and the dark prison of karmic fear and doubt.
- It will nurture titiksha in daily life.
- It will bestow resilience to transcend material limitations.
- It will remove ego from the equation of growth.
- It will allow for a marriage of pragmatism and spirituality.
- It will offer a long-term vision incorporating the self, family, community, nation.

The process of acceptance: Shreya or preya?

Poet, writer and civil right activist Maya Angelou explained the importance of courage of mind as follows, 'Courage is the most important of all virtues because without courage, you cannot practise any other virtue consistently.'

The ancient Kathopanishad elaborated on it with the concepts of shreya and priya—

Shreyash preyasch manushyametastau sampareetya
vivanaki dheerah
Shreyo hi dheerobhi preyaso vrineete preyo mando
yogakshemaad vrineete

This shloka states one must be able to distinguish between the nature of shreya and preya. Shreya refers to righteous action and preya refers to desirable one. Without titiksha, both will appear the same. Superior judgement/wisdom alone will distinguish between the two—mental strength is required to make the shreya choice, while avoiding the temptation of the preya one.

Why is this significant?

Because bountiful shreya is indispensable for divine joy and success; this is why the wise are cheerful and confident. It is not that their life is without adversity but they are skilled in navigating challenges. By making the elevated choice at each crucial juncture, not the desirable one, they cruise through entangled situations at the workplace and in personal life. Intellectual or emotional quandaries, personal or professional challenges—they exercise the choice of shreya displaying moral clarity, resolve and spiritual strength.

But one whose emotions are unregulated and senses overwhelmed, will find making this choice a tight-rope walk and will make the preya one. For instance, if—

- You believe I do not have time for anything or anyone—what you will possess is stress
- You believe I cannot achieve anything significant—what you will be consumed with is doubt
- You desire everything—what you will be overcome with is lust
- You believe I can do it all and by myself—what you will be left with is fear.
- You believe I should give up—what you will be crushed by is dejection

- You work without a plan or faith—what you will sense is chaos
- You work with anger or hatred—what you will receive is failure

A broad canopy of unconstrained emotions can and do overwhelm the decision-making process, when not guided by titiksha. But with a tectonic shift in the outlook, one can make the evolved, intuitive choice and unlock hitherto unknown dimensions of success and excellence.

Intuition, really?

Yes, although it cannot be measured its significance cannot be doubted. What I have observed is if I go against the gut feel, I end up making a wrong choice. Try to observe this in your day-to-day—if you have a visceral reaction or pick up a distressing vibe from a person or a project, know that they may contain hidden facets which have been detected by the wise subconscious. The reaction may not be a loud or overt, perhaps a tinge of discomfort but pay heed to it. Because it is a vital instinct honed over thousands of years of evolution, it shows up to safeguard us from concealed threats.

Early man used it to hunt and avoid predators and we can utilize it to navigate the burgeoning temptations of preya.

Knowledge and dharma: A synergy of success

Courage of mind is also required when knowledge and dharma come face to face. Especially when decision making is complicated by a multitude of factors amidst a climate of uncertainty and instability, what should influence the process—shreya or preya? Family or Community? Personal need or group goal? Duty or pleasure? Dharma or adharma?

Let's travel back to the distant past with the epic Mahabharata and examine the impact of a momentous decision influenced by a personal relationship during a period of great turmoil.

Karna, a celebrated warrior was the son of Kunti and half-brother of the Kauravas. Before the great war broke out between the Kauravas and the Pandavas, he was presented with two choices:

Shreya (righteous): To join the dharmic war of the Pandavas

Preya (desirable): To stand by his friend Duryodhana

Although a noble warrior, this set of choices clouded his intellect. Consumed by strong emotions, he chose to discharge the duty towards the friend. On the face of it, it appeared to be a principled decision—supporting a friend is dutiful, admirable but it was unbeknownst to him that performing the dharma is paramount.

In the grand scheme of things, he landed on the side of adharma, thanks to a misplaced sense of loyalty, and suffered defeat along with the non-righteous Kaurava clan.

Thus, Dharma or righteousness, the worthy companion of knowledge, should be the lone resort during a critical decision-making process. It may appear challenging but regular reflection on the nature of dharma and duty will enhance awareness, build conviction and strengthen resolve on this journey.

The Upanishads add—

> *Satyam vada,* dharma *chara swadhyayanma pramdadh satyanan*
> *Pramditavyma* dharma*nna pramdaditavyma*
> *Kushalnaan pramaditavyam, Bhutyai na pramaditavyma, Svadhyayapravachanabhyam na pramaditavyma*
>
> (Taittiriya Upanishad)

One must live a righteous life and pursue self-knowledge. Rightful action must be prioritized and adharma and temptations must be defeated with the awareness of the self.

Another example of the clash of emotion and dharma can be found in the pages of the revered Ramayana.

Before the war between Lord Rama and demon King Ravana, the Lankan princes had two choices.

- **Shreya(righteous):** To join the dharmic war against Ravana
- **Preya(desirable):** To fulfil the fraternal duty to Ravana

Kumbhakaran chose to support his brother believing it was the right thing to do-it was both a familial duty and a royal duty to the king of Lanka. When the younger prince Vibhishan attempted to persuade him to change his decision, he refused his counsel, although he was aware Ravan had committed a heinous sin by abducting Goddess Sita.

Vibhishan chose to discharge his dharma and although he was labelled a traitor, it was he who was proven right by history. For he was driven by shreya (standing up against a tyrant) while Kumbhakaran was driven by preya. This obfuscated his decision-making, forcing him to ignore the facts of the situation and the impending suffering of the innocent Lankan people due to the war foisted upon them.

Very clearly, in both the examples those who acted without contemplation of dharma suffered while the ethical achieved stunning victories victorious and continue to be revered after thousands of years.

With hindsight, it appears unexacting to arrive at this conclusion but personal equations and strong emotions can make the decision-making process go awry.

To summarize, the sacred union of dharma and wisdom supersedes the ego, the individual, and even destiny; it is guaranteed to triumph over adharma and ignorance in this age of Kaliyuga and artificial intelligence.

Practising the Acceptance Principle: Example of managing expectations and emotions

In the months preceding the visit to the Tirupati temple in Chennai discussed earlier, I had been working on a book for children. I had planned to offer gratitude during the pilgrimage, being confident that it would soon be accepted by a publisher. But as luck would have it, I received a 'no' and the next day, the opportunity arose to visit the temple.

Disappointed, I debated whether to go ahead. Why offer thanks for a no? But the sagacious message of the Acceptance Principle loomed over the mental horizon—accept win and loss with grace. Also, the message of Kintsugi flashed bright—accept broken pottery aka rejection as a piece of art.

It sounds poetic but did not feel so during the experience. After toiling for hours on a project, the fruit of rejection tasted bitter, and brought with it a Pandora's Box of emotions. How to accept the disturbing 'no' on my doorstep, or in this case, in my inbox as an alluring piece of art?

This salient question forced me to spend many moments in contemplation and led to the realization—why had I forgotten that I had been blessed with divine grace on scores of occasions? When I accepted them gleefully, should I not be strong enough to accept the no? Why should gratitude be conditional?

The outcome could not be altered; the no would remain a no. What was in my grasp? Only my sky-high expectations and attitude. So, I prepared the self to accept the situation and resolved to work harder in the future. Perhaps, there was a kindness hidden within the email, which could not be foreseen. Yes, I had wanted to offer gratitude for the assumed acceptance, now it would be for the clear rejection.

It was far from easy but I had to practise the Acceptance Principle in real life. But when I received another no after a few more days, I wondered why all the lessons had to be learnt at one go. Did I not need practice to accept 'yes' as well? I could not and did not want to accept the 'no's instantly—this is understandable as recovery cannot be immediate. As long as we can pick ourselves up on an acceptable timeline, it should be fine. It did take me time but I(sort of) have learnt to accept rejection as part of my journey as a writer.

That was/is my challenge as a creative person; I have to be open to rejection and criticism, however harsh or well-intentioned they maybe. And that is on a good day. On other days, when emails and proposals remain unanswered for, let's say, eons, it leaves one wondering if they were delivered to an other-worldly mysterious realm where computers/emails do not exist and/or were devoured en route by a voracious email-monitoring, fire spewing monster. The benefits of possessing a vivid imagination, I suppose.

Monster or no monster, I have managed to accept a negative reply or a lack of one along with the resultant self-doubt, without letting it hinder future creative pursuits.

For you, it may be a challenge wrapped in a discrete emotion; if you are a sportsperson, it may be the desire to secure a podium at every competition which will make loss unbearable; as an artist it may be managing expectations in the face of public apathy to a creative venture. As an actor or a blogger, it may be the trolling you receive for an experimental piece of work, as an employee it may be the dismissal/rejection of a recommendation or report; as a manager, it may be the cancellation of a dream project and as a homemaker, it may be the desire to meet the growing expectations of a tough-to-please family member.

In either case, acceptance is the way forward.

At a glance: Art of action/art of knowledge/art of devotion

The logic of the Acceptance Principle flows through philosophies, geographies and situations but remains timeless and relevant in every era.

Let's examine its impact on the three key routes to redemption: the philosophies of the Art of Action, Art of Knowledge and the Art of Devotion and observe how they influence decision-making.

Suffering/challenge

- **The manager/householder who adopts the art of action:** He will treat suffering as a fruit of action and will not be attracted or repulsed by it.
- **The one who adopts the art of knowledge:** Being rational, he will accept the cyclical nature of existence and treat suffering or challenge as an opportunity for advancement and character building.
- **The one who adopts faith:** He will accept suffering as a gift from the divine.

Joy

- **The manager/worker who adopts the art of action:** He will accept joy as a result of hard work and not over-celebrate it.
- **The one who adopts the art of knowledge:** He will treat joy as a fleeting emotion and instead of material pleasure, pursue genuine bliss.
- **The one who adopts the art of faith:** He will be ever-joyful due to his faith in divinity.

Growth

- **The manager/worker who chooses the art of action:** He will seek collective advancement and growth as it is his solemn duty towards the community.
- **The one who adopts the art of knowledge:** He will accept individual and group destinies as one so he will naturally pursue shared prosperity.
- **The one who adopts the art of faith:** He will seek communal welfare with goodwill and compassion towards all.

Collaboration

- **The manager/employee who adopts the art of action:** He will choose to work with the team as a form of duty—to himself, to his people and to excellence.
- **The one who adopts art of knowledge:** Being logical, he will accept efficiency and diversity will

result from team effort and will translate into sustainable accomplishment of goals.

- **The one who adopts the art of faith:** Accepting the Unity of Creation, he will nurture collaboration as the norm for progress.

Thus, we see the impact of the ever-wise Acceptance Principle causes real change in the mindset, irrespective of the doctrine adopted by the seeker. Galvanized by a vision of shared prosperity and peace, it ensures a thoughtful, superior choice in the face of mindless materialism and extreme individualism.

Luminaries who lived on their terms: Knowledge meets purpose and courage

Now let's take some real-life examples of mega intellectuals and witness the impact of knowledge, courage and yogic tenets including the Acceptance Principle on their lives. The multi-front accomplishments of these distinguished luminaries will highlight the fact that when knowledge meets purpose, there remains no ceiling on achievement.

Saint Gargi: Vedic scholar

Let's begin with scholar Saint Gargi, who shattered the myth that women were not educated or independent in ancient India. A shining example of a liberated mind, Gargi was a woman determined to forge her destiny and live by her rules in the ancient Vedic era. Her brilliance was evident from an early age—but it unsettled her family, who envisioned a more conventional path for her. Her mother gently urged her to abandon the pursuit of knowledge and, instead, suggested she prepare for a future centered on marriage. But Gargi rejected the path well-trodden and pursued her passions. She explored and researched on the nature of man, soul, creation and the metaphysical aspects of existence. Soon, she was accepted as a towering intellectual and was credited with contributing important hymns to the Rig Veda. Widely respected in the community, she was accorded the status of a Navaratna and considered one of the nine jewels in the court of King Janak of Mithila, the lone woman to be named so.

Her intellect was timeless, and her drive unmatched. Her dedication and excellence hold the power to inspire millions to pursue their dreams. And yet, her contributions have been forgotten—her story, quietly sidelined by history. Is it the researcher-historian bias which concealed her achievements or societal indifference which did not celebrate a woman breaking out of the pre-conceived mould? Perhaps both.

In any case, Gargi's life journey energizes us to stand up against the archaic norms of society, reject the stereotypes that cage ambition and deny agency to women. Hers was an authentic life; she accepted her gifts and developed them to the fullest. If she had followed the diktats of society, she would not have reached the dizzying heights of success she deserved. Tellingly, the art of knowledge demands sacrifice and perseverance but offers rich dividends to the earnest.

Chanakya: Advisor to Chandragupta Maurya

In contrast to the example above, Chanakya's (300 BC) storied life is well-known. An Indian economist, teacher and advisor of Takshila in the Maurya kingdom, his superlative treatise 'the Arthashastra' on Indian politics, economics and property is revered till today and widely accepted as grounded in logic and rational thought

As the unparalleled advisor to Chandragupta Maurya, the first emperor who unified India, Chanakya was respected for his sagacity and feared for his piercing wit. What's more, he was instrumental in guiding Emperor Ashok and in managing his vast kingdom, although critics have underlined his usage of trickery. The key was his understanding of human nature and ability to optimize royal resources, human or otherwise.

Vidura: Prime Minister of the Pandavas

Vidura, the Prime Minister of the Pandavas, was known as Dharmaraja, the king of righteousness. Skilled in diverse spheres, he was famed for his compassion and for placing the welfare of lay people at the centre of his philosophy, Vidur Neeti. It was he who advised the wisest of the Pandavas, Yudhisthir, against the game of dice and we know the devastating chain of events that were set in motion when such wise counsel was ignored. He was also the lone voice of reason(apart from Prince Vikarna) against the injustice meted out to Queen Draupadi. And he proved his dedication to dharmic principles once again when he chose the side of the Pandavas during the war of Kurukshetra.

Ahilya bai Holkar: The brave Maratha Queen

Ahilya bai Holkar(1725–95) was the Maratha queen of Indore from Chondi in Ahmednagar, Maharashtra. Against the social conventions of that era, she was educated by her father Mankoji Shinde, a commander in the Maratha army. After the demise of her husband, she ascended to the throne of the Holkar dynasty amidst stiff opposition but silenced her detractors soon enough. A virtuous ruler, she efficiently managed the affairs of the kingdom, leading the army to victory during many a war. Righteous and inspirational, she continued to work for the marginalized and revitalized the cultural essence of the kingdom with a transformative reign. Powered by intellect, resilience and charisma, her contributions transcended the barriers of gender, caste, creed, sect and hierarchy and today she stands as a role model of excellence and titiksha.

Saint Rahim: Eminent poet and noble

Sant Rahim was a well-known Indian poet and a noble in the court of Mughal Emperor Akbar during the 16th–17th centuries. One of his nine jewels or *navratnas*, his wisdom and spiritual insights are evident in his masterful creations which are relevant till today.

An intuitive couplet goes as follows—

Rahiman bole jaan de bahi
Jab se chete tab se sahi

Rahim advises one to let bygones be bygones. To 'Let it go'—similar to the song from the movie Frozen, for he believed when a mistake was committed unknowingly, it was better to accept it and move on. The best moment to restart was the present, not the next day or the weekend, as the river of life paused for none. The awakening, not the timing, was important, and the process of nurturing awareness was the right path for it.

Saint Kabir: Poet and mystic

A similar line of thought is observed in the intellectual works of the beloved Indian mystic Kabir who lived in the 15th century. His creations have been a wellspring of hope, inspiration and solace for the lay person, infused as they are with mystical relevance, wisdom and meaning. Many a contemporary concern finds its answer in them, which although belong to the distant past continue to be deeply relevant today.

For instance, a common enough question is on what basis should a wise person be evaluated? Kabir replied:

Jati na poocho sadhu ki pooch lijiye gyan,
Mol karo talwat ka, pada rahn do mayaan

That is, do not choose a teacher, influencer or guru based on caste, creed or appearance—these are outer markings or embellishments, which are immaterial. Centering religion, caste or sect during the process of growth achieves little—to gauge an intellectual's calibre, the depth and practice of their knowledge must be considered.

For instance, when you purchase a sword or to make it relevant to the modern seeker, when you select a smartphone, do you examine the features of the cover? No, you examine the sharpness of the blade or in this case, the features of the phone, number of cameras, processor speed, battery life etc. Or if you are an iPhone user, you may choose the next one as and when an upgrade is launched.

Will the phone cover serve the need or the phone? Will the cover of the sword be useful in the battle or the sword? So, it's the principal need that matters: Shreya, not preya; because the religion, caste, creed and sect are external labels on the self, like the cover of the sword or of the smartphone.

It's not that they are inconsequential; cool covers are necessary to navigate modern life but not without the smartphone holding them. Thus, the salient feature of his message is to go beyond the external facade for internal growth.

In the battlefield of life, a failure to distinguish between shreya and preya will lead to disorder and disarray. If we find ourselves armed with an elegant but blunt sword—or in this case, an intellect left unsharpened or outdated—we will inevitably pay a heavy price. Similarly, in the corporate battlefield, if one pays scant attention to mastering new skills, time management, innovation and quality management which are shreyic decisions, prospects of success will diminish.

Kabir explained this further:

Nahaye dhoye kya hua joman mail na jaye
Meen sada jal mein dhoye bas na jaye

Questioning the over-emphasis on the body, he said: What is the point of over-cleansing the body, while ignoring the thick layer of dust on the mind? When a fish is plucked out of water, it retains its scent. So, investing effort in the physical appearance alone while ignoring mental health is illogical and ignores the big picture. Eventually, the imbalance will lead to a collapse like the proverbial house of cards.

The barometer of societal growth: Honouring knowledge

What the examples highlight is that towering intellectuals like Saint Kabir, Saint Rahim, Ahilyabai Holkar, and Mirabai, among others, were revered in ancient times and continue to be honoured today irrespective of their caste, creed, religion or gender for a reason.

Because they sought to be the best versions of themselves, not a poor imitation of another. Because they accepted their authentic self, and were able to achieve their potential. Because they dared to accept their higher responsibility which may have been against social mores but which allowed them to go further than what was considered possible in their times.

And they did it all on their own steam, with *gyan* as their guiding light. Best of all, their pure wisdom was not merely for personal profit or in service of the elite, but deployed for communal upliftment.

Their philosophy, words, actions were not based on complex, abstract themes but were an embodiment of practical and spiritual knowledge. Aligning deed and speech, they were a living, breathing proof of a timeless philosophy, a sparkling truth which continues to touch the hearts of generations.

But what transpires when the wise are ignored or silenced, when their words do not match their actions, when ignorance clouds the horizon? A direction in which modern society is heading towards. Well, it is akin to sounding the death knell for the collective consciousness.

Jin ghar sadhu na pujiye ghar ki seva nahi
Te ghar marghat janiye, bhut base tin maahi

Here Kabir stresses on the importance of honouring the original thinkers, leaders and visionaries who can inspire and unlock a community's potential. Instead, if their voices are stifled, the community will slide into chaos and will be akin to a graveyard, a resting place for shared potential and abundance. That is, instead of critical, analytical and innovative minds, it will be populated with ignorant, melancholy spirits.

For when the voice of intellectuals is suppressed and their position usurped by self-serving ignorants, it will nurture a post-truth, post-reality society where facts will be adjusted, honesty vilified and candor derided. It will halt progress, create social fissures and lead to the downfall of the nation.

Thus, growth of knowledge and presence of independent, rational minds as a barometer of social, economic and cultural progress cannot be stated enough. The ancients understood this well.

Consider this—When swarms of marauding conquerors sought to uproot ancient civilizations, what ruinous strategy did they adopt? They burnt down cities, libraries and universities; all the repositories of knowledge including books, traditional knowledge systems, art and symbols of culture and heritage which anchored communities. Further, they silenced intellectuals, scholars and visionaries who could pose a semblance of challenge to their regime and ideology.

For instance, when the Nazis sought to impose fascism on German society, one of the inglorious routes they chose was the burning of books, destruction of art and the silencing/murder of intellectuals who challenged their imperialistic philosophy. This allowed them to rule over the country with impunity while dreaming of conquering the world.

Bringing Tenet 3 into life: Acceptance is power

As observed in the lives of inspiring intellectuals discussed above, deploying the stirring Acceptance Principle and titiksha is imperative to staying ahead of the curve in personal and professional life.

Pause and reflect- do you accept the wins and losses with grace, the highs and lows with patience and the yeses and nos with cheer? While accepting the downs and losses, do you chart a new course while avoiding the pitfalls of the old approach? Or do you allow loss to defeat you and keep you awake in the night? Do you attempt to find a new pathway to success, gently, without burning both ends of the candle, while forcing others to do the same?

Both in personal and professional life, a habit of self-reflection and analysis, planning and learning will help you discover the answers and realize your remarkable potential:

- Instead of blindly following others or doing the thing that is already done (preya), emulate the brave-hearted to chart your and your team's course (shreya).
- Instead of merely dreaming, make goals smarter, realistic and measurable.
- Instead of adopting the latest buzz words or trendy management styles, choose what works for your particular team and organization.
- Instead of networking/viewing others as resources to exploit, collaborate with respect and empathy.
- Instead of viewing the self as a machine and working non-stop (70 or 80 hours a week or whatever the latest trend is), approach the duty in a strategic, sensible, sustainable manner.
- Instead of classifying others as the enemy/rival and forming cliques like the old boys' club, accept diversity, inclusion, equity and sensitivity as the norm.

- Instead of fear or greed, accept work-life with a sense of gratitude, towards blessings small and big.
- Instead of dejection, accept the changing times and tides with patience, humour and grace.

FOUR

Tenet 4 of Gyan Yoga: The Higher Identity—The Consciousness Principle

In the preceding chapters, we discussed how self-knowledge inspires a life of authenticity and acceptance, freeing the self from the layers of ego and delusion. Just like an insurance policy secures the financial future, self-knowledge secures the intellectual and spiritual future, two aspects often neglected amidst the maddening pace of life in the Artificial Intelligence Age (AI).

As discussed in Tenet 2, the preparation for navigating and securing the future involves enhancing self-cognition-the first part elaborated on the basic nature and this second part leads the inquiry into the identity.

Inquiry into the higher nature: A reckoning with the self

Beyond memory, date or record, the inquiry into man's nature was led by ancient seekers, seers, saints, mystics and prophets. The intellectual milieu of ancient times was conducive for exploring the metaphysical, the mysterious, the magic of the spirit and the stars and resulted in the establishment of great philosophies and doctrines.

And today, the line of inquiry continues by modern scientists, philosophers, mathematicians and rationalists with life-changing internal and external expeditions.

But it wasn't straightforward then and it isn't now.

Why?

Because when I say 'I know something' or 'I want to learn something', it refers to information processed by the mind. As it is material in nature, it struggles to grasp the metaphysical and spiritual nuances of creation. What is witnessed at any point is a product of the senses, so it is not the nature of the true self. And for the untrained mind, it remains a dream within a dream.

The Hollywood blockbuster Inception elaborates upon the concept of dreams within dreams—on similar lines, here the real identity exists within the material, beyond the narrow dimensions of mind and matter.

However, para knowledge can illuminate the truth beyond dimensions and dualities.

In the cosmos, this duality presents itself in myriad ways—where there is wisdom there is ignorance, where there is mourning there is celebration, where there is victory there is defeat; where there is summer, there is winter. Material awareness is also a facet of material ignorance.

But the presence of this obvious duality does not obstruct the flow of cosmic truth detailed in Gyan Yoga.

An example will clarify this—

Picture your living room in the darkness of night; its

furniture is not visible. You know it like the back of your hand: it has a sofa, a table and probably a few potted plants. Can you confidently state they do not exist? You will not, although they are shrouded in darkness.

If you flip on a light switch, the furniture will come into view. Did it come into existence or in view? You know the answer to that. What about when you switch on a brighter light? Other things will come into view like the dust on the floor or the cobwebs on the ceiling which you have been promising to attend to for a while now, but which we will park aside for the time being.

Coming back to the pieces of furniture, you know they exist. What prevented you from viewing them? The darkness. Or the absence of light, which caused you to overlook things right under the nose. Remember gravity in Tenet 1—it exists but is hidden from view.

In the same way, the light of the being exists but stays out of sight because of the blinding darkness of ignorance. If the pursuit of knowledge came equipped with a button, we could simply switch it on and reveal the effulgence of reality but alas, that is not a possibility.

What is possible is that we can dip into the wisdom of ancient philosophy and drive out the darkness of ignorance to reveal the true identity.

The message of the Upanishads: The song of existence

After years and hours of rigorous analysis, intense dhyaan (meditation) and devoted sadhana or austerities, ancient Indian philosophers and sages of yore concluded there was an indivisible identity or truth at the core of existence, but it lay beyond the mind, the senses, the world. It was defined as the Consciousness Principle; it was and is the universal principle which defines existence, undergoing no genesis or destruction.

As the light of identity, it is the transcendent spark which elevates, energises and enlivens the being and is also referred to as *jeeva.*

Thus, there are two components to the being—the body and the soul. The mortal body is carbon based and by definition, prone to change. It is brought alive by the enduring Conciousness Principle.

So what are we really—the body or the consciousness? Where is this consciousness; where can I discover it, what is it made of and why can I not observe it?

In the beginning of the spiritual journey, one assumes—I am the mind-body.

Just as darkness convinces the mind there is no furniture in the living room, ignorance may convince one to accept this confining label. But if and when one advances, they will realize they are not limited by labels but are the sacrosanct Consciousness principle.

Does it require significant achievement or accomplishment to accept the self as the principle?

No, it requires not a physical transformation, but an intellectual one. Each being is already the distinguished principle in motion—they merely have to accept it. It does not require any struggle or strife, any clash or conflict, but profound awareness of the unadulterated, indisputable, inescapable truth.

Well, where does it reside?

The indomitable and indestructible Consciousness Principle resides within and is referred to in different ways in different cultures—as the soul, the spirit, the atman or the individual consciousness. Although its discovery is prevented by the dark shadows of ignorance, much like the furniture's in the aforementioned dusty living room.

It is described as:

Avinashi tu tadviddhi yena sarvam idam tatam
Vinasham avyayasyaasya na kaschit kartum arhati
(BG 2-17)

That is, the soul which pervades the body is known to be undying and is the incommutable power which controls the material body.

Who controls this controller? The Supreme consciousness further discussed in Tenet 5.

Let's return for a moment to the dim living room which we have promised to spruce up; we will discover three *tatvas* or facts contained within—

- **The *Bhogya*:** What is experienced
- **The *Bhokta*:** The one who experiences the experience
- **Brahman:** The ultimate reality or the supreme controller

Here, it was we who as the bhokta experienced the room, the furniture was being experienced, but there was a truth in the room which we were unable to witness.

It was the sublime reality of the Consciousness Principle, unwitnessed due to the darkness of ignorance of the self.

Nature of Consciousness Principle: A reckoning with truth

Our identity is thus—We are not the material body but the constant spirit which enlivens it. How does this work?

Take water for example. It adopts the shape of the vessel it is poured into. In a round cup, it appears circular, in a square cup, square and so on—water remains the same, without losing its individuality or identity. When you observe a cup, you accept it contains water—not square or round water, not juice or oil because of the change of shape.

Water retains its identity while adjusting to the vessel—it does not misidentify as a square or a circle, neither does it struggle to retain shape or colour. Similarly, we must remember that the mortal body is an earthly vessel into which the undying spirit has been poured into and that undergoes the unending cycle of birth, growth and death, while the mystical soul, the real identity, remains unaltered during the process.

Vasamsi jirnani yatha vihaya
Navanigrihanti naro parani
Tatha sarirani vihaya jirnani
Anyani samyati navani dehi (BG 2-22)

That is, as one puts on new clothes and discards old ones, the soul takes on a new body, giving up the old one.

This may raise a new set of questions (a sign of a waking intellect): why accept the transient body as the bona fide identity, that which is but a fleeting visitor of the ever-changing world, the one which grapples with mutations and material challenges? Why wage endless war over its unremitting needs? Why not accept the genuine identity as the one underpinning Creation?

On a rainy evening as I explored this tenet, it inspired me to jot down the following lines—

You and we
Are travellers of this realm,
And the next and the next.
Who knows what they will unveil?
Or what lies hidden between their layers?
Come, transcend the layers, the moments,
The nows, the nevers,
The heres, the theres
The whys, the hows,
The yeses and the nos.
And the cosmic game we witness,
As neither the doer, nor the enjoyer
Which plays us, which plays itself.

Key characteristics

Coming back, let's explore the defining characteristics of this higher principle.

After years of intense *sadhana, tapasya,* meditation and advancement in the art of knowledge, ancient seers perceived the presence of the Consciousness principle and described it as:

- *Nityaha*: It is the luminous one which existed before the beginning of creation and will continue to exist after its end
- *Satyaa*: It is what lends existence to another
- *Akarta*: It is not the doer of action
- *Abhokta*: It is the non-receiver of the result of actions
- *Acharah*: It is immovable
- *Sarvagataha*: It is all-pervading, it is everywhere at once
- *Aprameyaha*: It is never an object of experience
- *Santana*: It is limitless, free from boundaries or restrictions

To sum up, the consciousness is:

- Not a part of any material object
- Not a character or attribute of any object, including the mind-body
- Not a product created from a material object including the body or mind

Avyakto yam achintayo yam avikaryo yamuchyate
Tasmadevam vidit vainam nanushochitum arhasi

(BG 2-25)

That is, the soul is invisible, inconceivable, and immutable. Why grieve for the body?

Thus, it is not a part, product, portion, property of any object of the world, be it the body or any other substance. This makes the incandescent non-material, consciousness an independent principle pervading the entirety of existence. The base of life on earth, it is without limiting attributes or *gunas*: primeval, pristine and permanent. Enlivening and harmonizing the cells, it is the cardinal cause which allows the participants of Creation to interact with each other.

It shares its distinctive properties with all-encompassing Absolute Knowledge—both are never destroyed or created, not diminished as per location, purpose, listener or creator, and remain limitless, untarnished and unconquerable. Unbound by the laws of time, space, weight, they do not disappear and continue to flow in all epochs staying relevant, meaningful and purposeful. Neither are they perceived by the sense organs or by the ego and as such are considered invisible.

Awareness of the principle: Harbinger of truth

It is said the Upanishads had/have a sole aim—of revealing this epoch defining truth of the Conciousness Principle to every seeker. Hence, they are referred to as the prime source of *atman vidya* or self-knowledge.

Why was/is this truth considered vital to a seeker?

Much like the first ray of dawn heralds the end of night, it illuminates the temporary nature of the world and the fundamental eternal nature of the soul. Uniting these irreconcilable forces of existence, it balances the transient and enduring facets of existence and engenders a radical shift within, enlightening the mind and unburdening the self.

Indeed—
Wealth will take its leave,
Youth will bid goodbye,
Seasons will come and go,
Time will melt into the wind,
Karma will come calling,
But knowledge will shine on.
Consciousness and faith,
Will stay with and within forever.

Nasato vidyate bhavo nabhavo vidyate satah
Ubhayorapi dristontas tvanayos tattvadarshibhi (BG 2-16)

That is, the wise seers of truth are aware the transient (body) does not endure and the eternal (soul) does not fade.

Consider this: After the passage of the body (but before the last rites are performed), although it remains in an inert form, it is said the person is no more. Why would that be the truth if the individual was the body? Because subconsciously, one is aware that departed was the divine spark which enlivened it, and what it left behind was the mortal vessel containing it which reverted to its inert form.

Benefits of imbibing the Ceaseless Principle

It offers an evolved, independent identity

Well, if we are not the material body, the dynamic changes it undergoes do not apply to us. Birth, death, ageing, disease—they apply to the body but not to the cosmic self, thus it frees one from the multi-headed limitations of matter and the matter-based.

It also clarifies that carbon-based forms will continue to evolve but since the majestic Conciousness Principle is not derived from them, the changes will not reflect on them. This acute awareness frees one from mutations, modification and decay, empowering the self to go beyond material limits. As it ushers in acceptance of the past, present and future, it leads to the affirmation of the celestial self as the pure identity which does not undergo metamorphosis or lose existence.

This eternal nature of the Conciousness Principle is the cornerstone of spiritual existence and underlines the nature of the self as unchanging, undying and unending.

Since the principle is unchanging, so are you. Since it is blissful, so are you.

Since it is eternal, so are you. Since it is limitless, so are you.

Since it is fearless, so are you. Since it is undying, so are you.

Since it is independent, so are you. Since it is unbreakable, so are you.

It offers security and stability

Vedanta states that as the all-pervading consciousness, we must accept the self as the fountain of security, independence, eternity and stability. Since it is steeped in foreverness, the fleeting and the ephemeral will not offer much-needed stability. Thus, considering the material objects as must-haves and drivers of existence is a fallacy.

It is we who are the vivacious drivers—sovereign, formidable and fearless. We bring it alive and oversee its evolution as its incomparable, matchless creator. How can we be at the mercy of our creation? It is improbable. Why not accept we are much stronger than the bubbles of euphoria and sorrow it may direct towards us, hardier than the clouds of disease and sickness it may send our way and brawnier than the storms and squalls it may surprise us with?

Truly, the nourishing awareness of the Consciousness Principle offers refreshing stability and inspires acceptance of changing nature of the world.

If and when we disregard the limitless self, the Consciousness and the Authenticity Principles, we will be ensnared by *sansara*, a life defined by stress, fear, anxiety and instability.

It offers elysian freedom from karmic cycles

If I am the Conciousness Principle, you may wonder why perform dramatic karmas or care about future growth? This is a common question. Upon advancement, certain gyan yogis do not engage with duty and transcend work, world and worry.

Does it signify, the most knowledgeable ones amongst us can merrily abandon duty and twiddle their thumbs?

It would be a gigantic loss to humanity. In Tenet 2, we observed it was a spiritual duty to invest in the authentic potential. Post or prior advancement, all must continue to perform the duty whilst channeling the spirit of the wise. That is, engage with the honourable duty without attachment as the sophisticated intellectual. It will be considered akin to non-work when performed with surrender, without ego and by offering the result to the divine.

Otherwise, we will suffer the result of actions ensnared in the pre-ordained cycle of creation and destruction. It is only with the mindset of the *akarta* gyani we can sidestep the karmic quotient in spite of ceaseless engagement. We may follow in their footsteps, reject the illusive divisions of the world and continue on the chosen path.

Didn't enlightened souls including Swami Vivekananda, Mahatma Gandhi, Lord Buddha and Lord Mahavira remain dedicated to their mission of uplifting humanity, even after self-realization? They did not disappear into the distant Himalayas or abandon their duties although they possessed no selfish desires. On the contrary, their singular goal was collective salvation and they succeeded in elevating millions of lives with their extraordinary message of compassion, love, unity and peace.

Then, how can we ignore duty under the pretext of knowledge, how can we abandon ambition or progress? There is no excuse or reason to do so. Whether the duty is to the self or to the community, it cannot be shirked. It would be the opposite result of what we set out to accomplish on this terrain.

What about the saints that adopted renunciation on this path, you may wonder?

It is an individual choice and maybe suited to them. However, in the hallowed pages of the Gita, Lord Krishna clarified the renunciation of the ego was superior to the one of material possessions.

Thus, there is no excuse to avoid the duties towards the family, the workplace and the community. Whichever philosophy or path you may adopt, it must not include the abandonment of those dependent on you.

In this way, you will avoid the severe karmic impact which will accrue upon abdication of duty. Remember Tenet 2 shared the immutable karmas will travel over millennia, never retreating till the results are delivered?

Alignment with the Consciousness Principle, the sincere realization of the cosmic soul, acceptance of the fact that I am not the body, I am the sovereign principle in motion—these are inimitable routes to navigate them. They will offer true liberation, true moksha and true freedom from the clutches of sansara, and ensure union of the layers of the self.

Indeed, with the convergence of duty, devotion and deepened awareness, the progressive self can be united with the collective and finally with the supreme consciousness, the cosmic destiny of the soul.

Bringing Tenet 4 into life: Sources of inspiration

An example will clarify the process of imbibing wisdom—

When my son was around 5-6 years old, bubble sticks were his favourite. Initially when a bubble burst within seconds, he would be upset but after a period of time, he learnt to get over it. Now that he is older and wiser, if he ever plays with a bubble stick will he be upset if a bubble bursts? No, because he is aware of its short-lived nature. Who argues with a frothy bubble, anyway? But this acceptance came with age and maturity.

Similarly with time and experience, we must learn to accept the short-lived nature of the matter based, the evolving nature of the body and the permanent aspect of the soul. Why willfully reject the shelf life of matter which is much like that of the shiny bubble? Whatever is based on it, is injected with an end point. If it is present today, it will not exist tomorrow or in the future—accept the truth of the material bubble and realize the futility of chasing the ephemeral.

Continuing with an unhealthy dependence on the matter based generates instability, fear, greed, lust and stress will constitute a life of sansara. Of course, it should not be misconstrued as being uncaring towards the body, but a necessary step to avoid over-attachment. Wisdom dictates we take excellent care of it because it is a divine gift to navigate the challenges of life and a recourse to overcoming the karmic legacy.

We must also accept the infallible consciousness as the transcendent self, existing through all time, ever-luminous, ever-harmonious and evergreen.

Challenges of daily life may make us lose touch or create resistance towards accepting the nuanced reality of the Consciousness Principle. Then, we can seek sources of inspiration, in real life or on social media. But we must proceed with caution as a recent experience illustrated.

A few months ago, a friend posted an inspiring quote on her Instagram page and I messaged her to discuss it. She replied she was unaware of its meaning—she had plucked it from a website because it appeared mystical.

That is the desperate bubble of social media we had discussed in the introductory chapter: it is not all what it seems to be. An algorithm driven manipulative ecosystem, it places an inordinate amount of pressure on the lay person, forcing them to project an unreal image of themselves. Attractive but hollow much like a soapy bubble, it lacks essence and truth. But as the online community judges a book by its cover, appearances stay at the mercy of control c- control v—copy and paste.

Why blame the friend—who really has an illuminating quote to share every day? So we should view the online world as a mirage which flashes its own version of truth, which exemplifies the delusions and dysfunctions of the offline world and traps the innocent in an echo chamber of division and deceit.

Hers was an uncomplicated desire to appear philosophical to friends and followers but there may be some with an ulterior motive, who may leverage the process to influence and trick the gullible. Today, there are numerous influencers online and offline who spin a web of lies to increase likes, follows, shares for monetary benefits.

Without naming names, a handful of them have been exposed for falsifying backgrounds and credentials. Who knows how many remain and if they are paid to showcase dubious/harmful products and services? So-called gurus, experts, fake licenses and fraudulent degrees are a dime a dozen online.

Do we believe or follow everyone we run into in real lifesounds ridiculous, does it not? Then, why accept as the gospel truth what is shown on social media by an unknown source?

FIVE

Tenet 5 of Gyan Yoga: The Divinity Principle

'There is no difference between knowledge and devotion. The knowledgeable will worship the truth and the devotee with the grace of the Lord, will imbibe the knowledge of the Creation and both will arrive at the same destination, albeit from contrasting directions.'

—Saint Tulsidas

The fifth tenet of Gyan Yoga is the Divinity Principle which is defined as the underlying thread weaving together the fabric of the universe, the Consciousness Principle and the material elements of the cosmos. This principle is accepted as the undivided, singular, clarifying and defining force in play since the dawn of existence. Indeed, humanity has credited the Divinity Principle as the creative reality and force behind space-time, nature and jeeva.

However, religions and cultures have approached the principle in unique ways—worshipping deities, organizing religions, practising diverse rituals, rites and ceremonies—all the while claiming the superiority of their divinity. But on one subject alone, they appear to be in agreement. In the existence of divinity and of the supreme divine. They may refer to Him by unique names, but He alone is accepted as the source of creation.

He is the creator of the world, but He is not part of it. The creations are from Him and by Him, but He is not bound by them. He is the light which defines their existence but is not perceived by the untrained seeker.

In the previous chapter, Tenet 4 of Gyan Yoga stated the Consciousness Principle is infinite in nature. Well, it is believed, so is divinity. If the cosmos is created by divinity, it stands to reason that divinity influences consciousness too.

If we use mathematics to elaborate on this: if a=b, and b=c, then a=c, it signifies that since divinity is infinite, so is the Conciousness Principle.

The Gita adds:

Natvevahma jatu nasam na twa mneme janadhipa
Na chaiva nabhavishyaam sarve vayamata rparam

(BG 2:12)

That is, there was never an era when I or you did not exist, nor all the kings. Even in the future, we shall not cease to exist.

If both principles are verily infinite, can there exist two infinities? That would defy explanation. Infinity by definition is unbound, which never ends, which continues forever and ever. This gives rise to the existence of a singular infinity pervading the principle, the being and the world. This also clarifies that the unbound Creation is pervaded by the same principle and there is no duality. Admittedly, they appear non-identical but there is no separation of the consciousness—the universe is a clear expansion of the supreme consciousness and the individual consciousness is part of the greater collective.

This non-duality is the basis of the Advait philosophy established by Adi Shankaracharya which stated if there was no subject, there was no object, which signified the absence of duality. Thus, the Self, the Creation and the Other were one and the same.

Who is their creator? Of everything?

The Divinity Principle who is perceived to be the creator, nurturer and destroyer of this light-filled world and all worlds. In the Sanatana dharma, this divine energy is expressed in the trinity of Gods with Lord Brahma as the God of creation, Lord Vishnu as the God of preservation and Lord Shiva as the Lord of destruction. In Christian theology, it refers to the trinity of Father, Son and Holy Spirit, while in Islam, it refers to the all-merciful Allah.

The creator of yoga: Lord Shiva

Coming back to the Sanatan dharma, since yoga is believed to be imbued with divine, mystical origins, who is considered its sacred creator?

It is Lord Shiva who is worshipped as the supreme creator of the mystical art of yoga. As the essence and the base of all universes and the yogi of all yogis, his right eye represents the blazing sun, the left eye the luminous moon and the fierce third eye the fire of wisdom. Considered to be source of universal wisdom, it is His grace which pervades the world, dismantles sin and incinerates the karmic burden.

At this point you may be wondering, how the God of destruction can be the God of yoga? Because the word destruction carries a gloomy, unfavourable connotation. Well, look at it this way: destruction is the harbinger of new beginnings. It removes the attachment to the now and is the basis of creation of tomorrow, a pre-condition of growth.

By ushering in destruction, Lord Shiva blesses the material and spiritual existence with abundant, bountiful energy, priming it for growth. This allows the glorious Creation to flow uninterrupted even during its destructive phase. From the nothingness or the unmanifest, its seed emerges, it grows, exists for a brief period and unmanifests, only to manifest again in a new form.

A science student can confirm there is no destruction or creation of energy here (since it is not possible)—it is a cosmic dance which continues unabated.

Offering homage to the one directing these energies that is Lord Shiva, Saint Adi Shankaracharya, the spiritual leader and rationalist said, 'Forgive me, oh Shiva. My three great sins. I came on a pilgrimage to Kashi forgetting you are omnipresent. I'm thinking about you, I forgot that you are beyond thought. I'm praying to you, I forgot that you are beyond words.'

This ode to the ethereal cosmic dimension of Shiva aptly describes Him as one beyond word, pilgrimage and thought. Uncontained by the material creation, His unassailable force cannot be captured in words, and so no description of divinity can be considered complete.

Still, a divine Sanskrit shloka does attempt to detail Lord Shiva's mystical essence—

> *Karpura gouram karunavataram sansaar saaram, bhujagendraharam*
> *Sada vasantam, hridayarvinde, bhavam bhavani sahitam namami*

He is the one who is as pure as camphor, who is the embodiment of compassion, who is the essence of the world, who wears the garland of snakes, the one who is in bloom and the one who resides in me; I bow to both Lord Shiva and his consort Goddess Parvati.

Where there is Lord Shiva, there is Goddess Parvati and where there is divinity, there is knowledge; where there is knowledge there is compassion and where there is compassion there is love. This leads into to the concept of *Ardhanarishwar*, a unity of divinity which harmonizes the feminine and masculine energies, the yin and yang of the universe.

Driving the cycle of creation and destruction, the conjoined divine energies of Shiva-Parvati remain seamlessly intertwined in the fabric of the cosmos and define its existence by their overarching presence. Since times most ancient, this cosmic unity is expressed in the pantheon of Hindu gods in the form of Ram Sita, Radha Krishna and Shiva Kali amongst others

Goddess Kali's depiction is different from other gods. Although the consort of Lord Shiva is presented with a fury darkened face, tongue hanging out, and a fearsome garland of skulls in her hand, she is venerated as the Mother Goddess whose wrath is channelled only for the annihilation of evil. Her divine essence is elaborated upon as—

Jayanti mangala kali bahdrakali kapalini
Durga swaha shiva Dhatri swaha swadha namostute

She is 'Jayanti or the victorious one, she is Mangala or the harbinger of welfare, she is Kali, beyond time, she is Bhadrakali who controls life and death, she is the one who wields the weapon called Kapala to slay demons and she is the one who wears the garland of skulls. She is Durga, the Mother goddess, Shiva, the epitome of auspiciousness, Kshama, the ever-merciful one, the Dhatri, the one who supports the creation and Swaha, the one who receives the sacrifices—I offer my respect to you.'

Both Mahakaal and Mahakaali(Shiva and Kali) symbolize a signature blend of cosmic powers which transcend gender, space and material constraints. This eloquent unity of masculine and feminine divine energies is evident in the intricate choreography of creation—as a dominant force which controls all forces including time and space. Thus, they are the past, present and future but also beyond them. Controlling and annihilating the very essence of kaal and karma, their divine expression and sacred identity pervades, defines, creates and nurtures the created and the creation.

Oh, do you believe time is the most dominant force in the world—are these not oft-repeated—time is money, it heals everything, it is king? But time is a human construct forged to demystify the comings and goings of the world. How can it be more powerful than the one who is all-sustaining and all-knowing?

Goddess Saraswati: The goddess of knowledge

The salience of the feminine divine on the *marga* or path of gyan is further illuminated by the position of eminence held by Goddess Saraswati. Worshipped as the embodiment of wisdom, speech, arts, music and purification, she is also accorded respect as the goddess of water which symbolizes its immense purifying powers.

The daughter of Lord Brahma, the creator of the universe in Hindu epics, Goddess Saraswati is venerated as the benevolent mother, an ode to her nurturing side, and as the source of unparalleled knowledge, unrivalled strength and untameable ferocity, a tribute to her warrior-like personality.

The trinity of goddesses Lakshmi, Saraswati and Parvati in Sanatana dharma celebrates the enduring, all-encompassing power of the divine feminine. As a form of the mystical Goddess Shakti, these goddesses are considered the source of incalculable power coursing through the heartbeat of the cosmos and through the veins of every being.

Beyond time and space, and beyond masculine and feminine energies, their persona and powers make it abundantly clear that knowledge is not the exclusive preserve of an era, gender, orientation, caste or class of people but the birthright of humanity.

Ya devi sarvabhuteshu ma Saraswati rupena sansthita
Namastasye namastaye namastasye namo nama

The mantra by Rishi Vak, describes the omnipotent and omniscient persona of the Goddess. She is the one who is present in all matter, who is omniscient, who is present across eras; I bow to her, I bow to her and I bow to her again. The personification of proficiency, she is the Goddess who existed in the past, is present in the now and will be present in the future. She is our past, our present and the gateway to our future.

The exalted position of goddesses in Santana dharma categorically refutes the misconception that knowledge, progress or success come attached with a ceiling, glass or otherwise.

Nature of divinity: A return to identity

Single or numberless, form or formless, feminine or masculine—the nature of the Divinity Principle was addressed by the conclusive teachings of the Upanishads and summed up as the Brahmn, the reality of existence and the source of knowledge.

The Gita shloka explains the nature of Brahmn—

Brahmarpanam brahmn havir bramhaagnau brahmana hutam
Bramhaiva tena gantavyam brahmna-karma samadhina
(BG 4-24)

The process of offering is the Brahmn, that which is offered is the Brahmn. Sacrifice is offered in the fire of Brahmn and is attained by those who see Brahmn in all action.

The Gita adds:

Etad yonini bhutanisarvani tupadharaya
Aham kritsnasya jagat Prabhava pralayastatha (BG 7:6)

All have their source in the spiritual or the material. Of them both, I am the origin and the supreme cause of annihilation.

Thus, Lord Krishna proclaimed He was the creator of the world and the source of every object in the Creation and advised transcendence as the path to realizing the nature of Brahman:

Brahma Bhuta prasannatma na shochati na kaksati
Samah sarvesu bhutesu madbhkatim labhate param
(BG 18:54)

One who is situated in transcendence will realize the Brahman. He will never desire or lament to possess, he will be the same to all and will attain devotion to Me.

The chief aspects of the nature of divinity are:

- **Divinity is indivisible although worshipped in myriad forms**

'Different people take the name of God by different names. Some people say Allah, some say God, some say Shiva, Krishna, Brahma, it is like the water filled in a lake. Someone drinks water from one side of a lake and calls it *jal*. Others drink from a different bank and call it *pani*, and some people drink it from a different place and call it water. Hindus call it *jal* and Muslim called it *pani.* But it is the same thing.'

The words of Sri Ramakrishna Paramhansa, a revered saint and the guru of Swami Vivekananda clarify divinity cannot be divided. Fundamentally, it remains unchanged but when viewed with a dissimilar perspective, presents itself in an altered form. That does not recast its essence or indivisible nature.

For instance, rose tinted glasses will make the world appear pink. To all others, it will appear as it is. We may argue it is pretty and pink and would be right but the others arguing against us, would be right too.

- **It is the absolute truth and absolute goal of existence**

The ancient sages of the universe declared divinity as the absolute goal of mankind, tthat there was and is no greater truth than divinity, no bigger freedom than its awareness and no better accomplishment than its acceptance. They hailed it as the indisputable knowledge factor, the noblest of all truths pervading every element of the cosmos and the absolute force infusing life with mystery and magic.

- **Its forms are manifold and symbolize eternity**

  a. *Para swarupam*: It is the form of divinity not conceived by the mind. Formless and without attributes, it is impeccable, perpetual and immeasurable.

b. *Vyuha swarupam*: The form of divinity accepted as the cause of creation, preservation and destruction.
c. *Vibhava swarupam*: The form of divinity who arrives in avatar form to root out evil and restore dharma.
d. *Antaryami swarupam*: The form of divinity residing within the heart of devotees.
e. *Archa swarupam*: The form of divinity presiding as the idol in the temple or at home.

- **It is infinite and without definition**

Its nature is considered definition-less, but paradoxically it is the one which defines what being human means.

- **The principle is omniscient and omnipresent**

The Gita describes the Divinity Principle as the *kshetragya* or the knower of the *kshetra*—He is the supreme force influencing the universe and the jeevas. As the all-enduring and all-present principle, He is the undisputed cause driving action, energy and life cycles and ensures the consciousness is at work across the playground of the world. Existing in eternity and beyond, He is the omniscient and omnipotent factor of the cosmos.

The playground of the world is referred to as the kshetra, the universal field of operations created by the divine kshetragya. In it, dwell the living beings, the farmers who sow the seeds and await the harvest season. What are these crops? The dominant karmic heritage, the result of actions performed in the spirited, fertile kshetra.

Kshetragya chapimam vidhi sarvashetreshu Bharata
Kshetra ksetragya yor Gyanam yat taGyanm mata mama

Lord Krishna said, 'I am the Knower (kshetragya) in and of all bodily fields, and understanding the body and the Knower is the process of knowledge.'

Thus the nature of the Divinity Principle can be summed up as the indivisible, the absolute, the definitionless and the all-knowing force of existence.

But what if one does not believe in the existence of divinity? Atheists and rationalists do not believe in organized religion and their gods and goddesses but in the cold, hard logic of science, so what does science say about of divinity?

The knower and the known: The paramount and the pilgrim

Science and spirituality have co-existed harmoniously in Indian and Eastern cultures, and where one ended, the other continued. What has also remained constant is that, be it religion, science, mathematics, physics or philosophy, the best of intellects across cultures and continents have continued to enquire into the nature of divinity and as an extension of that, into the nature of life.

So, let's head to the land of quantum physics which delves into the nature of consciousness. As you may be aware, Quantum Physics, founded by Max Planck and Neil Bohr, studies the behaviour of small particles which make up matter. At an atomic and sub-atomic level, they consist of electrons, protons and neutrons. How they behave was explained in the Uncertainty Principle propounded by German scientist Heisenberg; the principle states both the position and momentum of the particles cannot be accurately predicted, that is, if the position of a particle is known, its momentum cannot be predicted and vice versa, hence the name.

This offers a brief glimpse into the unpredictable behaviour of matter at the smallest of scales, and attempts to unveil the mysteries hidden within them. Such as, what are we made of, what is matter composed of, what is consciousness, where does it exist and what is it that make us, us?

Thanks to advancements in Physics, we know we are composed of atoms which consist of electrons, protons and neutrons. All beings crafted from matter consist of them but what is matter derived from?

In the words of scientist Max Planck, 'I regard matter as a derivative from consciousness. We cannot get behind consciousness. Everything that we talk about, everything that we regard as existing, postulates consciousness.'

He believed that matter was derived from consciousness and attributed it to a singular force. 'All matter originates and exists only by virtue of a force. We must assume behind this force the existence of a conscious and intelligent mind. The mind is the matrix of all matter.'

On similar lines, Einstein said, 'A human being is a part of a whole called by us the universe, a part limited by space-time. He experiences himself, his thought and feelings as something separated from the rest, a kind of optical delusion of his consciousness.' Einstein believed in the existence of a Unified Field theory, which would bring together all the laws of physics under one overlying principle that would offer an elegant explanation of the working of the universe but was unable to finish it before his death.

Other neuroscientists believe the cerebral cortex is the seat of consciousness while some quantum physicists lay stress on the existence of a universal form of energy perceived as intelligent and aware.

Although droves of scientists, atheists and rationalists do not believe in the concept of divinity or consciousness but it is interesting to note the progress of quantum science, quantum biology, technology and intellectual theories towards uncovering the answers sought since the advent of civilization.

Divinity in motion: Role of religions

As mentioned earlier, to demystify the inconceivable force behind the creation, and as an extension of that, nature and life, lay people used simple methods. So religions were organized, rituals laid down, books scripted, poems scribbled, voyages embarked upon and traditions established. To begin with, they nurtured the lofty aim of uniting the collective consciousness but soon each group began to assert its supremacy over the other. (Not the dreaded, inscrutable other again!)

From their legion of followers, they demanded uncritical submission, a non-questioning outlook, and total, blind compliance. This is contrary to the intuitive journey of Gyan Yoga or the pursuit of any form of knowledge. The relentless pursuit of knowledge demands a curious nature, a critical outlook, a chronic habit of challenging assumptions, quiet moments of self-reflection, a meaningful process of debate and constant exploration.

In any case, arguing about the superiority of religions is a pointless, self-defeating exercise. Can one divine force be compared to another? Can one infinity be bigger than another? If a certain portion is removed from infinity, will it cease to be infinite? Infinity will remain infinite. But causes of discord need not be.

Why can we not enrich the collective consciousness with the wisdom of all religions and prophets of the world? Religions and festivals can play a key role in minimizing the impact of the othership philosophy. Offering a rich repository of traditional knowledge systems tried and tested by ancient communities, they can unite and revive jaded hearts with a sense of shared history, identity, continuity and purpose.

Welcoming the Vignaharta: The god of wisdom, the son of Lord Shiva

Let's explore the wisdom enshrined within the festival which celebrates Sanatana dharma's Elephant God Lord Ganesha, Ganesh Chaturthi.

On this auspicious occasion, Hindus bring home a clay idol of Lord Ganesha, who is worshipped before all Gods, underlining his prominence in the divine hierarchy.

As per the tradition of various communities, the festival continues for 1.5, 3, 5,7 or 10 days and includes the *arti* or the holy prayer performed with flowers, fruits and fire.

But isn't idol worship contrary to the logical, rational thought process which most gyan yogis wax eloquent about? Why worship a piece of clay? Well, after it is established in line with traditions and rituals, the idol is considered akin to the divine. This symbolizes the deep power and promise of devotion.

Post this, worship and celebrations begin at a personal and community level with colourful cultural programs honouring the deity of new beginnings and the divine remover of obstacles to success. A scent of optimism and a spirit of gratitude infuse the air but soon, it is time for *visarjan* or the process of bidding farewell, a bittersweet day tinged with emotions.

So, what are the learnings this festival offers? Yes, it is not just for gobbling sweets although that is a deliciously important aspect.

The primary one being just as clay transforms into divinity, our bubble-like dreams can transform into reality. We are forms of carbon, remember. Perhaps, we should not be in a hurry to write ourselves off. Doesn't a mixture of earth, water, fire and ether lead to a Buddha and a Gandhi? When we can accept their transformation, we can hope for ours as well. We know what we are capable of, of the cathartic *yatra*s or quests we have undertaken and the fractious eras we have faced. Then why can we not accept the solemn promise of potential, the soft whisper of faith, the reassurance of a better tomorrow?

The second learning is that festivals can bring communities together in a spirit of camaraderie and divert focus from the unending needs of the self to the burgeoning needs of the collective. They have the power to unite devotees of diverse backgrounds and outlooks, reawaken the connection with divinity and each other. Also, also offer much-needed moments of solace and sustenance along with opportunities for reflection and renewal.

The third learning they impart is the importance of accepting the impermanent. What will come, must go, bittersweet or not. The wheels need to keep turning for the cycle to move. This is the rule of life—the blessed idol must return to nature at the poignant end of the festival. But after that, will come the return, so there is no cause of lament.

This is true for all journeys—the coming and goings will continue albeit in new forms and accompanied by novel set of experiences. These vagaries of life must be welcomed irrespective of what they will bring or take away.

The festival of Christmas

Another fine example is the festival of Christmas which celebrates the birth of Jesus Christ, who is worshipped as the son of God in Christianity. A spiritual, religious and cultural affair celebrated across the globe, it is a day of beauty, piety and joy, honouring the tradition and culture of the respective regions. It embodies the universal values of love, goodwill, and compassion, and serves to unite communities.

Indeed, festivals of all religions are designed to bring communities and hearts together, irrespective of rite and religion, culture and caste, ethnicity and indigeneity.

This message of universal brotherhood propagated by festivals and religions is elucidated upon by Sri Ramakrishna: 'I practised each religion for a time—Hinduism, Islam, Christianity. Furthermore, I followed the paths of the Saktas, Vaishnavas and the Vedantists. I realized that there is only 1 God towards whom all are traveling but the paths are different.'

Surely, if we journey together with knowledge and compassion,

We can and will discover unity, and divinity.
But if we flow with divisive ignorance,
We will discover the other, and bigotry.

Bringing Tenet 5 into life: Liberation with divinity

The Divinity Principle inspires one to ask—Why should we allow ourselves to fall victim to the machinations of division and discord? Instead why can we not problem solve boldly and deploy religion, culture and tradition to achieve unity? Why can we not seek to be independent architects of destiny? Why do we allow the othering process to prevail? Why can we not prevail, instead?

This process of advancement of thought will face challenges and distractions, each more complex/attractive than the other. Some may be trivial, others perfect storms whose blame will land on the doorstep of the other. But the passage away from these storms of ignorance exists.

My grandfather used to explain it with an example—

Consider the yellow sun rays as a twisted rope—since they are attractive, we may agree to be bound by them. After a while and perhaps a change of heart, we may realize we are caged, albeit in a prison of ignorance, but a prison, nevertheless. There are two routes to emancipation here—either become stronger and destroy the braided rope or shrink in size and escape its stifling constraint.

Consider the most blessed of devotees and the most prominent of intellectuals, Lord Hanuman. What route did he choose to gain undifferentiated success?

Route 1: Outshine and outperform the problem

When Lord Hanuman, an advanced gyan yogi, was captured by Lankan soldiers, the legend goes he grew in size till he was towering over the island kingdom. Unable to withstand his expansion, the constraints snapped of their own accord—this is symbolic of the divine path of Gyan Yoga.

Imperishable, inestimable, all-encompassing wisdom empowered the gargantuan form of the Monkey God to tear down the suffocating constraints of ignorance and ego, illuminating him with faith and heroic confidence. With the divine behemoth as a generous source of inspiration, we too can attack the wiry threads of ignorance binding the intellect, and ensure they are lying in tatters at our feet.

What is the intrinsic nature of this thick rope of ignorance?

It is illusory and bewildering: a form of mystifying maya, a projection of the false ego and a peculiar form of delusion which binds and eclipses the mind. But we can fight for freedom, like the supreme devotee did. We are free in any case—all we have to do is accept it. Why choose to live in an open-air prison of delusion? Instead, let's choose freedom——the first step is to realize the chains and the prison exists.

Oh, do you believe, 'I am lost, I cannot find myself, I don't know anything, I'm helpless and hopeless, I need someone else or something to find or rescue me.' This harmful self-talk has far-reaching ramifications; indulging in it will merely fan the hungry flames of ignorance and shatter self-worth. You are not a toy or a pencil box to be misplaced; you are exactly where you are supposed be at present. But you can gain momentum and reach where you seek to be in the future. Remember tenets 4 and 5—you are the Consciousness Principle and a spark of the Divinity Principle.

Woefully, we are unaware of the existence of the ropes of ignorance, doubt and fear. Or maybe we do not want to let them go because we are terrified of what horrors lie on the other side. This is why we run pillar to post for solutions, for success, for redemption, for divinity, never realising they reside within.

Route 2: Complete surrender of ego

The first route was to outmatch the problem while the second is to surrender the ego.

When he wanted to escape the clutches of Surasa who guarded the turbulent Lankan sea, Lord Hanuman shrank in size, zipped into her mouth and before she knew it, flew right back out. In this way, he stayed steadfast on his mission and honoured the boon granted by Lord Brahma that all travellers had to pass her mouth on that route.

This is emblematic of the shrinking of the divisive ego—the natural outcome of the path of devotion and knowledge.

In both routes, we observed the intellectual devotee weakened the ego's stranglehold on the self. In the first instance, the enhanced intellect resulting from Gyan Yoga overpowered and outclassed the binding delusions while in the second instance, unalloyed faith defeated the ego and secured success.

The two processes although multi-hued, helped Lord Hanuman arrive at his goal while offering unfading calm and unvarnished contentment. They anchored his luminous faith and melted away the shackles of material limitations, offering success in the face of unconquerable peaks and marine monsters.

The Gita says one who knows the destination reached by the art of knowledge is the same as the art of devotion witnesses the truth.

For the modern seeker, choosing either or both the paths will offer illimitable knowledge to transcend the impact of worldly events and the dynamic waves of destiny and division. Upon advancement, they will transform into a colossal who can bend the cosmic laws to their will. As an indestructible phoenix, they will rise from the ashes of the potent karmas to craft an illustrious future unchained, unlimited and undominated by the past or the present.

This brings us to the message of the last tenet. It is the Aham Brahmasmi principle.

SIX

Tenet 6 of Gyan Yoga: The Aham Brahmasmi Principle

In the preceding chapters, we observed the dance of existence expressed in the dualities of the permanent and the non-permanent, the then and the now, the primeval and the present, the sky and the shore, the I and the other.

Who made this observation?

Well, the mind. As discussed earlier, when the mind views the shore and the sky, it recognizes them as such because their memory exists in the brain. It is both the observer and the observed. Yet it is bound by material limitations and easily beguiled by maya—the winds of delusion and ignorance masquerading as fact. To move beyond these illusions, the mind must shed the thick layers of ignorance that obscure reality.

Without that, the individual in a maya-led delusion grip will consider the body as the primary identity. However, when this illusion is lifted, the identity of the self will be established. What is the essence of this creative identity?

The Upanishads explained it simply as Aham Brahmasmi—I am that. Aham—that what is inside. What is inside, the Consciousness Principle. Brahmasmi—divinity.

It is the summit of self-realization—when an individual awakens to the profound truth that they are what they have been seeking all along. That there never was, nor is, any separation between the self and the Self.

It is the moment of infallible self-acceptance and impeccable awareness: *I am infused with divinity. I am what I seek. I am a spark of the divine—indeed, divinity personified.*

How can one arrive at this summit?

It is possible to arrive at this natural conclusion, which lies beyond the gates of mortality and materiality, with the eternal art of Gyan Yoga. However, for a beginner seeker who is at the first rung of awareness, this may appear inexplicable.

For instance, take a wooden table—

The one with basic awareness will identify it as a mere table. The one who is knowledgeable will classify it as a piece of furniture made from wood. Only the one with enhanced wisdom will view it as a material object, prone to change.

Now take a lay person: He or she may identify the self as Mr Robin Cook or Ms Virginia Woolf (as per the body and given name), unaware of any other reality.

After imbibing knowledge, they may discover the existence of the Authenticity Principle and upon further advancement may strive to realize the Conciousness Principle. With further advancement on this path, they may come to accept the self as Aham Brahmasmi, the ultimate identity. It is a gradual process of removing the layers of ignorance which will bring one to the central tenet of truth.

How can one prepare the self for acceptance of this true identity?

By managing the nature or prakriti, that is its *ahankara* or the ego and mamkara, the feeling of ownership. The mind-body senses are a part of ahankara—they are essential tools to navigate life but are a cause for sansara. When a seeker identifies with them (due to a lack of awareness of identity) it leads to fear, helplessness, frustration and failure, text-book definitions of sansara.

Why? As an ahankara, one defines the limited self as a *karta*—doer, bhokta—enjoyer or *gyata*—knower. But all these roles emanate a sense of insufficiency and inadequacy.

Power of the principle: A cure for sansara

The Aham Brahmasmi principle soundly rejects the limited identity and the abject dejection they emanate. It defines the inner cosmic nature as neither the doer nor the enjoyer but as the unblemished witness.

Free from the myriad insecurities of sansara, such an elevated witness considers the self as one with a mortal body and an immortal destination. The result is an unvanquishable thought process liberated from the burden and baggage of life.

Who is this Aham Brahmasmi identity applicable to? All of the beings, some of them or none of them?

Gyan Yoga states supreme divinity pervades the universe. It is in you, in the neighbour, in a stranger, in a loved one and in nature in the form of flora and fauna. This shimmering truth lies at the heart of creation—it is built by divinity, from divinity and represents divinity.

This was also the base of the previous tenet which may bring up the question—Is knowledge divine or is divinity knowledge? Well, both of the above. Divinity is perceived to be absolute knowledge, which originates from a divine source. Their shared goal is the union of the self and the Self, the very definition of yoga.

To reiterate, it is not just your community, country or members of your religion who are divine, sentient beings, who are the principle in motion but all communities, all people. Divinity cannot be artificially constrained to a tribe, an auspicious place or a chosen people or time period; it pervades every element, every molecule and every being.

Essentially, this signifies there is one tribe, one world, one truth infused with divinity. We may be distinguishable but are all Aham Brahmasmi. This is the resplendent truth which underpins the working of the ever-expanding universe, which man has struggled to comprehend since the beginning of time and which is the sublime identity, the stately abode of the seeker, mystic, philosopher, poet, artist and the ever-curious mind.

Instrument of divinity: A source of peace

However, the materialism of the Digital Age is bursting with insidious desires, the sense of ownership and false ego which threaten peace and clarity.

Vihaya kamanya sarvanpumams charati nisprihaha
Virmamo nirhankaraha sa shantim adhigachati (BG 2-71)

That is, one who has given up desire for gratification, who has given up a sense of ownership and is devoid of false ego, will be the one to achieve peace of mind. Thus, the Gita clarifies without abandoning harmful desire one cannot ensure real peace.

This does not mean one should deny all desires and dwell alone on a barren peak. Such a dedicated monk or hermit will also possess the desire of propagation of knowledge, hunger, safety and so on. Thus, downright denial or desire annihilation is not practical or desirable but their conversion, reduction or management is.

Desire is not destiny, one can aim to grow out of it. Public accomplishment or private victory—this is true for both.

Let's explore the process of management of a simple desire. For instance, there may be some who nurture a sweet tooth and when I say some, I refer to yours truly. One fine day, if I decide to cut out sweets from my diet, what will happen? By personal experience I can confirm, the first few days will be somewhat distressing yet uneventful but the urge to enjoy a dessert(or two) will return shortly and ensure several are consumed at once. What did the process achieve—except ensure the mind was in turmoil?

A better approach is to manage the desire of consumption—to educate the self about the adverse impact of excess sugar, so that the desire to consume it diminishes. The aim is to weaken the pernicious desire, not the mind. Gradually after weeks/months of effort and self-talk, the attitude will shift, the habit will break, the craving will reduce, and the attachment will wane. Soon, it may be weeks before the desire of indulgence returns—I may face sweet bumps on this road but sluggish progress is also progress.

This, I believe, is a healthy way to grow out of desire—to loosen the hold of the object (or the desire) over the self and to reduce one's interest towards it. Not by brute force or threat. Then the overwhelming desire of owning them or the threat of them owning us will decline and we will gain a sweet new freedom.

The goal being to reach a stage where one can draw the sense organs away from the source of temptation—

Yada smharte chayam kurmo Gyaniva sarvasha
Indriyaninindriyyarthebhyas tasya pragya pratishtitha (BG 2-58)

The Gita says one who can draw his senses away like a tortoise draws itself into his shell is in true consciousness.

Naturally, an advanced seeker is in control of the senses; they are able to pull them away at will. It can be achieved via:

- A gradual, systematic process; not extreme measures
- By nurturing self-knowledge
- By un-chasing every desire—whether related to junk food or junk thoughts
- By navigating the lust of ownership and attachment, through sharing, donating and avoiding hoarding
- By curtailing the ego

Impact of accepting Aham Brahmasmi

The classical *atman gyan* of Aham Brahmasmi offers peace and purpose to the discerning seeker. A source of infinite unity, it erases the multiple sources of division and sansara and unites warring hearts and minds.

As it expands the self-identity beyond the worldly labels of mother, daughter, sister, friend, wife, mother, writer, teacher, dancer, a non-marathoner and so on, it mitigates stress, confusion, conflict and anxieties. Instead, it offers a universal identity which is beyond the plains of the self-proclaimed tribal, social, national and cultural identities. For its foundation, linkages and intuitive ties offer reassurance, meaning, purpose and liberation to the modern mind tormented by material burdens. Freed from such constraints, it shifts into the realm of the spiritual and the metaphysical, accepting a higher identity as the truth. Encircling the intellect, it surmounts the fear of the transitory nature of the universe, and of the seemingly invincible foes of illusion and delusion. It also deepens the connection—

- With the self
- With the divinity within
- With the world and
- With the Self
- And offers absolute liberation

It clarifies:

- We all are responsible for the fate of humanity.
- We possess what we need to flourish, without resorting to division.

- We all deserve to live in peace and prosperity.
- We must preserve the living legacy of our ancestors.
- And we must create a future where growth will knock not only on the doors with the 'right' identity, wealth, ethnicity or connections, but also on the doors of every community, gender, caste, religion and nation.

Imbibing the knowledge: Guru-Shishya tradition

The process of imbibing the tenets of Gyan Yoga is through the *guru-shishya parampara* or the teacher student tradition, a relationship revered in Indian culture. Because the guru is the custodian of knowledge and the personification of the divine, he is the sole instrument of liberation available to the seeker. Only with his grace and blessing can the *Bramha Swarupa,*or the divine incarnation behind the delusion of maya, be unveiled.

In the hands of an accomplished guru, information, raw details, tenets and philosophies with transformative potential can be mined, analyzed and applied. So that they manifest into destiny, and transform the seeker into a spiritual and intellectual powerhouse.

A guru's teachings ensure:

- ***Jeevan mukti*:** An existence of liberation from the pressure, division and ego inbuilt in life. It leads to the dawning realization that material limitations are created by the ego.

- ***Videha mukti*:** A state of purposeful eternity with no further births. All the karmas, even the most arcane ones are set ablaze, offering renaissance, resurgence and revival.

Who is the most revered of all gurus who can ensure this intellectual transition?

In the Gita, Lord Krishna is declared as the guru of all gurus and the distinguished charioteer of the world. As the Divinity Principle, He represents the supreme intellect which guides the heart, mind and spirit in the decision-making process.

Taddwid pratipaten pratiprashnena sevaya
Upadeshyanti te Gyanam gyani nastatvadarshinaha

The Gita states you can imbibe the Supreme Truth with the help of a guru. By approaching him with respect, you can master *atman gyan* and quell your doubts. For there will be a sizable number—both doubts and challenges.

Challenges in journey of Aham Brahmasmi

Saint Tulsidas cautioned the trail of knowledge grew exponentially harder in the face of life—'To follow the path of knowledge is to tread on the edge of a sword.'

The Gita adds—

Indriyanam hi charatam yam manonuvidhiyate
Tas asya harati prgyma vayur navam ivambhasi (BG 2-67)

As a gusty wind pushes away a boat in the water, any one

of the distracted senses can affect the intellect and distract one from the goal.

Surrounded by temptations, hurdles and distractions aplenty, a seeker must safeguard the spiritual, intellectual and metaphysical self against the following challenges—

It will be a foggy beginning

The radical odyssey of self-knowledge will not come with a detailed map. In the absence of a guru, one may not be unaware of the process or the destination. Even with one, it may not proceed as per plan, or life may get in the way. However, do not wait for all the pieces to fall into place. The fear of perfection is a tale spun by the mind—the ideal day, idea, project or moment does not exist.

It is important to understand that each moment and day is ideal and complete. If we wait for a specific moment, we will be locked in a prison of doubt. Initially, the details may be nebulous, but the ideas will come. Progress may be languid, but even that should be encouraged. Trust the inherent creativity, instinct and potential of the self, they have propelled growth well enough so far, why will they not in the future?

When I am planning a book, it begins with a seed of an idea. The whole book is never mapped out—that would be a dream come true, but who has such luck? No, really, I would like to know which author is so blessed. However, as long as I know the direction I'm heading in, I can find my way through the forest of words. Writers have unusual problems but so do other professions?

Some writers who dabble in fiction have shared they do not wait for the story to come fully formed to them. They begin with strongly etched characters (their personalities may be based on real people) and allow them to evolve through the pages—their goals, motivations and dreams take the plot forward organically, rather than a contrived collection of incidents.

Thus, even if the vistas and plans are foggy, plod on. The superfluous, the tempting and the ambient noise will gradually fade away and the gritty, disciplined and persistent approach will reap rewards.

An ancient tale outlines the benefit of this approach—

Once Guru Drona, the royal guru of the kingdom, invited the Pandavas and the Kaurava princes to shoot the eye of a toy bird in a distant tree. This was a test of archery, focus and analytical strength. When Pandava prince Arjuna was asked what lay in his vision, he replied, 'Only the target'. While other warriors were distracted by the pleasant surroundings, he remained focused and succeeded in his goal. No wonder, he was lauded as the best archer and one of the finest warriors of all time.

It will be a lonely road

Yes, the pathway to discovering and accepting the luminous identity will be paved with loneliness, misgivings, missteps and anxieties, one which you will have to walk alone, with doubt plaguing your every step.

Fortunately, the words of Rabindranath Tagore, the unparalleled visionary and thought leader, offer inspiration—

Jodi tor daak sune keyu na ashe
Taube ekla cholo re
Ekla cholo ekla cholo ekla cholo ekla cholo re

This lyrical Bangla poem continues but its sunny message is as follows: When you invite others on an expedition, and they don't respond, continue walking. Take your fear, uncertainty and doubt along. More often than not, it will not be a frictionless exercise. It will be a daunting, lonely walk, but that should not deter you. Rather, you should be ready for such an eventuality. Some may even offer discouragement but you must keep advancing in your orbit.

When the earth travels an impressive 2.6 million kms in a day, how can you stagnate? A few alike minds will join in eventually; you must welcome them because if you want to achieve a goal, you will need helping hands.

The herd mentality

Another example may take this further:

Have you heard of the annual wildebeest migration which unfolds in the heart of Africa? One of the few wildlife migrations on such a mammoth scale, the stunning landscape of Tanzania and Kenya comes alive with more than one and half million wild animals traveling thousands of miles at the end of the monsoons in May/June in search of water, food and safety. A cyclical ritual performed for centuries, it is an unbelievable spectacle that guarantees the safety of the multi-generational herd. In the animal kingdom, this moving phenomenon demonstrates the cycle of nature which works astonishingly well for the migrating beasts.

This is what we've seen and absorbed in the human kingdom as well: there is safety in numbers.

You can remain cocooned within the comfort of the herd, sure—but your bold streak, creative spark, and authentic self will always yearn for the unexplored and the uncharted. For the places others hesitate to venture to.

So, what should you do?

Question the need to follow the herd. And follow your own head.

Sure, it is easier to follow s when the route is pre-determined and the risk of the unknown diminished. But nothing new was discovered or created by doing the done thing or by blindly following and never leading. It may be lonely to begin with but will be rewarding when you discover greener pastures.

A similar situation was faced by young Indian graduates in the early 80s and 90s. Then, except for the public sector, there were two professions to choose from engineering and medical. Although things have changed now, then every child chose between the two, often with unhappy consequences. How is it plausible that millions of children with varying aptitudes were interested in a set of two pre-decided careers? It is understandable to be influenced by successful predecessors but there can be other routes to fulfil the destiny, than to choose or be forced to choose the path well-trodden.

It will require intentional effort

Acceptance of the identity and nurturing the true potential can bridge the gap between potential and performance, but between dreaming for the stars and day-dreaming, there exists a fine line. But it may as well be a murky moat filled with voracious piranhas. Couple of sub-optimal moves and it is game over; a tad dramatic, but clarifying nevertheless.

What I want to stress upon is that the vision of the future must be based on an accurate comprehension of the authentic potential. Then, building the base with clarity, curated goals and intentional effort will create a life of abundance. You cannot rest on the laurels, be lulled into a sense of complacency or await divine intervention. Unless you help yourself no one else will; prayer also works in conjunction with purposeful effort.

For instance, if you dream of success, but do not invest subsequent effort, you will not succeed even if you possess a world of knowledge. You need an executable action plan to bring it to fruition. Dreams need to be tempered with truth and backed by clarity, effort and logic, not fantasy, bluff or wishful thinking.

To sum up, foggy, lonely, laborious, it will be all this and then some but it will be an adventure worth embarking upon. For the journey to the awe-inspiring Aham Brahmasmi principle with its authenticity, abundance and bliss will bring the seeker to the hallowed truth of life. Then, the seeker will not remain a seeker—why would they continue to seek and pray, what would they seek?

With the expansion of their intellect, they will come to accept the self as the manifestation of the cosmic truth, above and beyond the narrow definitions of ignorance and material knowledge.

Transforming and transcending the cosmos, they will emerge as the source of unity and scorch the differences and divisions carved out by materialism. Their individual consciousness will expand, their ego will dissolve into eternity and integrate with divinity. At the sacred destination, they will emerge as the personification of the universe and the personification of truth, with a promise of eternal, blissful existence.

Unlocking the energy of universe and self: The promise of eternity

Can two words, Aham and Brahmasmi, be so potent and life-altering? Do you doubt the massive power and the fundamental knowledge hidden within them? Remember the explosive power of the inconsequential pebble of ignorance? We underestimated it to our detriment just as we love to underestimate the self.

But we cannot underestimate the power of science which ushered in the Atomic Age. Let's see how.

In physics class, you would have come across the famous Theory of Relativity proposed by Albert Einstein.

E=mc2—it expressed energy as a sum of mass and the square of the constant.

The speed of light is a constant in the universe, at 186,000 miles per second; nothing moves faster than it. When it is multiplied with matter, the sum is an astronomical amount of energy from a miniscule portion of mass.

Mass and energy may appear distinct, but are one and the same. It took a game-changing equation to reveal the staggering secret they had been silently harbouring. This led to the creation of the atomic bomb and the development of nuclear power plants which generate clean energy by the fission or splitting of atoms.

The energy, the atoms and their protons and electrons always existed—what changed? Science arrived on the landscape to unlock their potential. This is similar to the Mount Everest example; it always existed but needed a daring adventurer to scale it first.

In the same vein, the 'I am that' or the Aham Brahmasmi principle on the spiritual horizon has the capacity to unlock the infinite energy and infinite truth of the being by clarifying the relationship between pure consciousness and the truth. As it offers a meditation on life, reality, existence and truth, it heralds the being as a veritable force of nature and highlights the linkages between the elements of creation, existing at a much, much deeper level than has ever been comprehended.

With new theories that posit the creation is a conscious system, they shine a spotlight on the quantum aspect of life and the living being. Since consciousness is believed to be quantum in nature, approaching the individual as an eternal, non-material phenomenon offers a fresh perspective on creation and evolution, identity and self.

Although some may discount the self as an insular, inconsequential, fleeting dot in the vast expanse of the cosmos lacking the intense glamour and mystique of dark energy/ dark matter, it has the capacity to burn brighter than the most flamboyant supernovas and the most luminous stars, if it ultimately accepts the quantum nature: 'I am the light I so acutely crave, the creative source I so eagerly desire and the source of wisdom I so ardently worship. I am who I am seeking.'

If you still struggle to accept this, why not draw inspiration from the ocean's blue waters, rhythmic waves and cyclical tides, and observe the self as:

- **The eternal principle:** As you welcome a sea of experiences, rise and fall, recede and swell, flourish and flow with the tide till the goal is achieved.
- **The limitless principle:** Why not strive to reach the point where the mesmerizing waves do not affect poise and direction? Amidst the choppy waters, hold onto the higher identity and sail with unstinting belief towards the goal, aided by the limitless potential.
- **The fearless principle:** Why allow inclement weather to play spoilsport or allow the boat to capsize—storms do not last, fortitude does. Do not be overcome by pride when the surging waves offer a rippling embrace, neither be crushed when they unceremoniously toss you back on shore.
- **The knowledge principle:** How should you embark on this fierce voyage of self-discovery and growth? While sailing with ribbons of hope amidst the lapping waves, enjoying the call of the mercurial seagulls as the cool wind ruffles the hair; or while berating fellow passengers, ignoring the azure

views, the expansive menu, and while complaining endlessly about the salty sea breeze?

- **The blissful principle:** Just as the rising tide lifts the serene ocean, accept the elevation of the self as a steady source of joy. A wave in the ocean is the ocean itself; can the two ever be separated? Similarly, accept you are the blissful principle in motion amidst the waves of the world, away from the alternating, transient troughs and crests of joy and sorrow.

The outlook of the advanced seeker: The unbecoming

Akin to the process of unlocking energy from matter, this journey of knowledge, this journey to unbecoming, will free one's quantum potential from material constraints.

What is the mindset of the intellectual who arrives at this destination? How does it reflect on their outlook?

Arjuna posed a similar set of questions to Lord Krishna—

Kair lingais trin gunana etan atito bhavati prabho
Kimachara kahtam chaitamstrin gunan avitartate

(BG 14-21)

Arjuna asked: What are the internal changes by which I will know that I have transformed into a gyani? How will this reflect in my day-to-day behaviour? How did a gyani become one?

In Shloka 22, Lord Krishna replied—

Prakasham cha pravtrim cha mohmev cha pandava
Na devasti sampravtritani na nivrittani kanksati
Udasino vadasino gnaiyyo na vichalyate
Guna vartanta ityeva yo vithastathi nengate
Sama sukha dukkha svastha sama lostasma kanchanah
Tulya Priya priyo dhiras tulya nindatma samstutih
Manapamanayos tulyas tulyo mitrari pakshayo
Sarvarambha parityagi gunatitah sa uchyate

When one does not dislike illumination, attachment or delusion and neither hankers after them, they are deemed wise. When they remain undisturbed and unshaken while the *gunas* or attributes fluctuate, they are deemed wise. Their external environment does not alter the internal one; they look upon a pebble and a gold ornament with equipoise.

How do they react to the sweetness of praise and honour and the bitterness of blame and dishonour?

They accept both with grace; they are not emotionless, but resolute and resilient. Disallowing ignorance from taking root, they brush past the dualities of life to thrive in the present. Neither the regret of the past or the paralyzing fear of the future prevails over them. Pragmatic and persistent, their indefatigable mindset transcends the fluctuating modes of nature and the shadowy illusions of time.

Liberated, they do not struggle against the challenges posed by the material body or by fellow Homo sapiens—a species often inclined toward division. At last, they accept a simple truth: they were born free, and they remain so. Secure in their wholeness, completeness, they do not seek bliss from material creations but are content in the absolute knowledge of the self, the Brahmn and the identity.

Their mindset is described as—

Apuryamanam achala pratishtthanam, samudramapah pravishanti yadvat
Tadvat kaama yam pravishanti sarve, sa shantim apnoti na kaama kami

(BG 2-70)

Underwhelmed by the mists of desires, they are an ocean of knowledge steady in spite of receiving the torrential waters of raging rivers. Eternally peaceful, they remain unaffected by the strong currents of temptation and time.

In Shloka 26, Lord Krishna answers the third question—

Mam cha yovyabhiicharena bhakti yogena sevate
Sa gunan samatityaitan brahma bhuyaya kalpate

The destination of the gyani and the devotee is similar—the platform of *brahmbhav* which is oneness with divinity and consciousness.

Who is the transcendental Brahmn, the reality of the world?

Bhrahmano hi pratishtaham amritasyavyayasya cha
Shasvatasya cha dharma*sya sukhasyaikantikasya cha*

(BG 27)

Lord Krishna replied: I am the embodiment of Brahmn in my real nature. I am immortal and the source of happiness and eternity. You will become one with me.

He reassures Arjuna and all seekers that the constitution of Brahmn is eternal, indestructible and blessed. This transcendental destination can be reached with ease by the eminent gyani, the deft navigator of space-time and the keen traveller of the cosmos and the quantum world.

Bringing Tenet 6 into life: Flourishing with the higher identity

This shining truth of Aham Brahmasmi connects the individual consciousness to the grace of the creation and serves as an engine for individual and communal growth. It inspires acceleration in the direction of shared progress, but the world may pull one in an opposing direction. Problems ingrained in material existence may create delusions and lead one to question the truth and the purpose of the journey. Falsehood and delusions are lamentably widespread and may appear to win but one must hold onto the transcendental identity.

For even with upstanding karmas, you will have to face your fair share of challenges. This may be the result of accumulation of disagreeable karmas over manifold births. As discussed in the previous chapters, we are responsible for what we did in all the births, although we may have no recollection of them. It will make us question the necessity of taking the high road while others trudge down shady alleys.

How should we proceed?

With the inspiring shloka from the Upanishads—

Satyameva jayate nanritam
Satyena pantha vitati devayanah

(Mundaka Upanishad)

The truthful alone will win, not the deceitful. The truth offers a divine key to success—reflect on this and continue to advance.

As the light of the spiritual world, the wise must stay unshaken and distinguish between the truth and the non-truth, question age-old assumptions, refute superstitions and challenge the status quo. But do not expect change to flow instantly. The journey to knowledge is slow but steady, difficult but worth embarking upon.

Let's correlate it with the concept of return on investment. When you invest an amount of money (or effort) in a blue chip stock, you receive *y* amount of interest (profit, income and/or recognition) upon the completion of a project or time period. This is called return on investment. In a stock market, you may earn sizable returns, when the value of, say, a blue chip stock rises after a period of investment.

But when there is no immediate return of investment, what do the finance experts recommend? 'Don't exit the investment—it may become a profit-making proposition in time.'

In many ways, this mirrors the journey of accepting life's truths: the returns come with patience and persistence.

In the beginning, you may not see an uptick in returns, or enjoy big benefits. The terrain may be harsh, lonely and punitive, the texture of growth slow, almost unnoticeable but continue to stay invested. The aesthetics of sustainable growth and progress will bear fruit in the long run.

It must be said the performance of duty, ethics and a life driven by excellence and knowledge is not for the faint-hearted. Many have and will abandon them after receiving no tangible, instant benefit. Translation: no wealth, success or fame in the short term. But hefty benefits will accrue in the long term, although at a glacial pace. Do not be a rookie investor, ok?

If you exit the market without understanding its movement, you will lose the exciting returns around the corner. Similarly, if you go against your nature and karmic duties and abandon the righteous realm, you will suffer the full wrath of the cycle and lose out on future benefits.

Another example may illustrate it better—

Climate change matters. If we do not plan for the future, we will be left with a future we did not plan for. Logical but not delightful.

This is what the unfolding of the climate change saga demonstrates.

Most of us are aware the fossil fuel economy is impacting global eco-systems, but if we still exhibit reluctance toward the adoption of green alternatives, it will signal an awareness devoid of the foundation of wisdom.

But if an increasing number of leaders, decision makers and individuals consider it an investment offering incredible returns long-term, then we may see appreciable progress. Otherwise, without earth, where will their business be conducted? The example of attitudes towards climate change management symbolize the age-old struggle between shreya and preya discussed in the pages ahead.

True, decision making and implementing change are perceived to be onerous; but isn't everything notoriously difficult in the beginning? In the long-term, it is the only way forward—we do not need to be spiritual, gyani or a radical seeker to comprehend this. Anyone with a logical bent of nature can see the looming dangers on the horizon, only a materialistic, ignorant climate skeptic will ignore or deny it.

Be it war or climate change, both illustrate the presence of blinding ignorance inbuilt within the beastly nature of materialism. Destructive and dangerous, their blistering repercussion includes the eventual destruction of the planet and its inhabitants. Still believe ignorance is bliss?

It is no longer an if scenario but a when scenario-when we set climate change in motion, we ensured it was not my or your problem, about this or that country, my or your air or water, this or that war, mine or your community, this or that ideology, or about the good community or the dreaded other. It is about all of us, all countries, all beliefs, all clans, all tribes, all people—the collective consciousness.

To address the crises affecting humanity, we need to come together as a single consciousness but as history has shown, it is simple to divide, difficult to unite.

The tenets of Gyan Yoga and the metaphysical Aham Brahmasmi principle can nurture unity amongst communities, bringing all into their infinite, limitless, fearless, unending and blissful embrace. Doubtless, dateless and deathless, they offer unparallelled strength and light, heralding the uniting truth as a force of nature, a force of the cosmos and the divine force of existence.

Elevating the nation, community and the individual, they lead to the unequivocal declaration of the liberated, realized self—I am the subject of the inquiry, I am the truth, I am knowledge itself.

I am.

PART C

CONCLUSION

Looking Ahead: Embarking on the Natural Journey of Humanity

As we come to the end of this brief introduction to the peerless path of Gyan Yoga, it becomes abundantly clear why it has continued to resonate with mystics, intellectuals and seekers across the boundaries of space and time.

Hopefully, as more seekers choose to embark on this wondrous journey of peace and perseverance, it will unite bold minds and exemplary ideas across boundaries and borders and offer exposure to cross-cultural philosophies, audacious stories and intrepid adventures with unending possibilities. Which in turn will awaken the collective consciousness and enhance the understanding of the universal human experience with discussion and dialogue, reconciliation and restraint, hope and harmony, and peace and prosperity, sorely needed in these most divided of times.

This inscrutable era has converged challenges of all magnitudes and forms—think war, pandemic, climate change, and economic, social, technological and cultural provocations. In such a post-truth, post-fact, post-reality world, the future appears covered by a fog of delusion, blurring the line between truth and falsehood.

As we peer into this opaque future, questions new and old, profound and prosaic abound. Some have been already answered while some remain—How do we want the shared future to look like? In the AI era, which is already upon us, how can we craft a trajectory of growth which is just and equitable? And how can we harness the power of knowledge, both human and artificial, while contributing to the collective reservoir of intellect, amongst others?

Much will depend on how we choose to answer them. Mistakes may and will abound and as life is a laboratory, we may experiment and tread with caution till we find firm footing. But one hopes, it will be sooner rather than later. Already, we have stumbled into battles, skirmishes, civil unrest and wars which have become deadlier and more complex, thanks to the advent of technology.

Strangely, the more we modernize, the more we regress.

The more we innovate, the more we hate.

The more we create, the more we destroy.

The more we progress, the more we 'other'.

Always, the result has been loss and more loss, so elevating the thought process with the art of knowledge needs to be the way forward. It will be a gritty, gut-wrenching process but one with a bright light at the end of the tunnel.

Think about it. Would you choose to go to war against yourself? I hope not. Did that make you chuckle—

imagining an Olympic style wrestling match with you as your opponent? That mental image does lend itself to hilarity. Now, turn your attention back to the present. What do the tenets of Gyan Yoga state—all individuals are quantum beings crafted from the same divine soul and matter; the perceived separateness ungrounded in reality.

During war one is, for all intents and purposes, fighting against the self. How prudent should war-mongers and fear-mongers consider themselves? Will they be proud of winning and losing against themselves, after tearing down their neighbourhoods, culture and heritage? Perhaps, but their appalling behaviour defies logic.

Over thousands of years, every king, pharaoh, chieftain and leader waded into bloody wars when faced with a political/religious/social/financial conflict. They fell prey to the othering mindset and in turn, preyed upon hapless souls. So tormented were they by the ghost of the 'other,' they sought to exorcise it by war. Although, the radical idea of peace was not unheard of, it was considered inconceivable, indecipherable; perhaps the very thought sent shivers down the spine of most, except for a few notable exceptions.

The warrior king Ashoka the Great (268–232 BC), the third Mauryan Emperor of the Magadha kingdom in ancient India, was one. Upon assuming the throne, he waged the Kalinga(modern Orissa) war, one of the deadliest conflicts in the history of the sub-continent. But after a Pyrrhic victory, Ashoka was overcome with remorse over the scale of devastation and destruction, and dedicated the remainder of his life to peace. Inspired by the teachings of Lord Buddha, he renounced violence, war and the concept of 'the other', earning him the sobriquet by which he is known till today.

This has not been replicated enough.

Seeding knowledge: Me against the world to I am the world

Unfailingly over the course of history, global and community leaders have found a tribe or two (or more) to be at loggerheads with, because they are desperate to discover the mythical, fabled 'other'. War and division are everywhere as a result.

Because they are conditioned to think along those lines, because they know not there is no other. But the other also commits the same calamitous mistake, leading both to wage war endlessly.

In this digital era, as philosophy, science, technology and artificial intelligence intersect, this bigoted outlook should have been a relic of the past. But its root causes are ignored in infancy and so, it sauntered into adulthood, expanding its circle of influence, bringing a plethora of nations, communities and lives into its spate. It tugs away at the fragmented, fragile fabric of civilization, wiping out that which is precious and sacred.

Moreover, this is a never-ending geopolitical process. Today a country, let's call it A, is the ideological enemy, tomorrow it will be B. When the first nuclear bomb was designed, it was aimed to be a deterrent to the Nazis, who were the designated enemy of the era. Where was it used?

In Japan, the *other* enemy. After that, surely peace flourished? No. What came next was the Cold War between the USA and the erstwhile USSR—the *newer* enemy. The balance of power kept shifting, and so did the identity of *the other*.

Today, political leaders are wary of North Korea, China and some others, tomorrow it will be another set of countries.

Worryingly, the existence of war will never diminish unless it is understood to be a part of a dangerous cycle of othership and hatred. In this distressing equation, an aggressive, divisive outlook nurtured by ignorance plays the role of the constant which travels at the speed of light much like 'c' in the Relativity Principle. As it rushes to infects minds and harden hearts across boundaries and borders, it drags out and intensifies conflicts, turning them into unpalatable, incomprehensible multi-year (decade-long) feuds with socio-economic, religious and political issues that reinforce one other.

This me vs. the other and me vs. the rest of the world attitude will recur on loop, lest the eclectic tenets of the Art of Knowledge are established and imbibed. With them, a pathway to peaceful and prosperous co-existence and gasp, maybe even collaboration and unity is possible.

A shining example exists. The International Space Station (ISS) with its principals Russia, Canada, Japan, Europe, US is an example of what can be achieved with a collaborative spirit. Since its establishment in 1998, the pioneering station has played a pivotal role in disease research, drug development and space exploration. How did this miracle take place? Nations which are at each other throats on earth getting along swimmingly in the stratosphere and the great beyond?

If replicated in other sectors—enduring peace, climate change mitigation, poverty eradication, medical advancement so much can be achieved. But, no, on earth we busy ourselves with the spectacle of war. Just as Greek mathematician and physicist Archimedes had a Eureka moment when he discovered the principle of buoyancy, let's hope we and our leaders will have an epiphany too.

An ancient yet radical way of thinking

How about a radical thought experiment to get started? Consider the world as yours, for a minute. Not just the family, neighbourhood, or state, all the people, as yours. All the chosen and non-chosen ones. The other state, caste, religion and community as yours. All the countries. All the gods, too. The Supreme, too. He belongs to everyone, and everyone to Him.

This is the thought process behind the Sanskrit phrase *Vasudhaiva Kutumbakam*—the whole world is one family.

Was that too radical? Probably.

Then, why not take a smaller step and begin by honouring the right to life for all? Along with the right to shared growth opportunities? The ones you take for granted for your tribe. Was that also an uphill task? Can you at least wish for no harm to another? Now, is there a stir of compassion for their people, apologies, your people?

Without the fig leaf of ego, it is possible to think along these lines, worship at the altar of oneness and overcome the illusory fear of the other. As observed in the preceding chapters, with the exuberance of titiksha and the Unity of Creation one can discover common ground, forge unity and express solidarity with all players on the stage of the universe.

To initiate the next chapter of growth and to navigate the uncertain AI age, this is imperative.

Nurturing the green roots of wisdom

Yes, effecting change will not be straightforward.

As an individual and as a community, it will be challenging to think along these lines and weave in 5000 years of sublime wisdom into the nuance of thought and action.

As economic, social, intellectual, cultural and geopolitical realities collide, even deeply ingrained attitudes can evolve for meaningful societal change, when preceded by an unfettered exchange of ideas.

The knowledge traditions of ancient and modern cultures, from India or Japan, China or Africa, from the East or the West, are a heritage of humanity, a treasure worth protecting. They can heal the shared psyche, the cultural soul and intellectual landscape of the collective. Why not adopt them as a stable bridge between borders, between the past and the future, the material and the spiritual, the individual and the universe, the human and the artificial? Why not honour and practise them till they leap off from the pages of history and into our lives.

The winds will shift, so why not begin to *aekla cholo* for now? As you begin, remember to clear out the pesky cobwebs from the living room of the mind and the dusty pebbles of ignorance from the river of your intellect.

Then, continue to trust the inner voice, lead the herd, scale the mountain, offer gratitude, grow the business, delight the customer, make better choices, navigate short-lived bubbles, climb that mountain if you must, run the marathon (or not), and witness life transform into play and play into life.

Of course, there will be no low-hanging fruits rather this is a life-long process, and may bring a barrage of disruption but you have to be fearlessly persistent, unapologetically effective and absolutely resilient to usher in change.

Every effort will be successful when paved with the intention of peace, growth, discovery and unity. As you advance, you will throw off the yoke of fear weighing you down and stand up for the self and the other. Undoubtedly, this evocative process will pull down the walls of hostility and division, offering renewal and redemption.

As it elevates the mind and strengthens the relationship with the individual and the collective consciousness, it will ensure prosperous growth through a creative, intellectual and spiritual churn.

Seekers, yogis and leaders, both ancient and modern like Saint Kabir, Nelson Mandela, Gandhi, Gargi and Swami Vivekananda succeeded in doing so on this path and their journeys stand as a testament to the universality and relevance of knowledge. Their elevated outlook and lives of excellence offer a call to action, a direction of growth, an opportunity of discovery and a forward path to success.

We can emulate them—along with the journeys of Saraswati and Kali; Chanakya and Shiva; Gargi and Queen Lakshmi Bai, Krishna and Buddha or any other leader of our choice. Immersed in their spiritual stream of consciousness, we can savour the fragrance of their intellect, nurture identity and rejoice in the realm of the collective consciousness. Indeed—

You are Saraswati when you enrich the intellect,

Kali when you fight your demons,
Gargi when you dismantle doubt
Durga when you defeat fear

You are Chanakya when you drive destiny.

Shiva when you transcend time
Krishna when you inspire the spirit
And Ram when you lead humanity.

Nature as a divine teacher: Connection and hope blooms

I am optimistic that the idea of us as universal seekers and immortal beings walking and transcending unexplored frontiers will ensure the magical intermingling of heaven and earth, of the ancient and the ageless, of the material and the spiritual.

During this fulfilling journey, we can also seek inspiration from the humbling magnificence and cosmic artistry of nature.

The awe-inspiring splendour of the Northern Lights or the Aurora Borealis, the show-stopping beauty of the thundering Victoria waterfalls, the snowy peaks of the majestic Himalayas, the life-giving waters of the Nile river, the carbon-rich forests of the Amazon and the brilliant arm of the Milky Way lighting up the indigo sky, amongst others: they express the mystical wisdom of nature in a scintillating manner and are crafted in quantum knowledge as we are.

It is the grandeur which defines the mysterious spiral galaxies with contain millions of stars.

The spiral which is found in sandy sea shells, which although miniscule hold the roar of the ocean within.

The glorious roar which defines sweeping hurricanes which quieten to a whisper as they depart.

The soulful whisper which carries a hint of poetry, the chromatic verses signalling a new dawn of hope.

The fresh dawn which paints the sky pale-blue with gratitude and meaning.

The tender blue which paints the placid sea and brightens the curious eye, the window of the soul.

The same sacred soul which is in every being—inter-connected, in motion, in balance, in grace.

Illuminating and inspiring, astonishing and abundant, speaking the languages of lives lived, smiles shared, mistakes committed and lessons learnt, they define the inter-connectedness of the self and the Self, of universe and nature, while offering a lesson in abundance, creativity, wisdom, balance and excellence.

Going ahead, in this climate of hybrid wars and hybrid work, our knowledge sources must be hybrid too. Whether we choose the boundless universe, the rough seas, the soothing birdsong, the tropical rainforests and/or the constellation of stars, both philosophical and scientific inquiries are available to us. All we need to do is open the heart with hope and humility and imbibe their secrets. Who knows, we may discover the wisdom of life, the cosmic truth and the nature of the consciousness dissolved in the atom, in the photon, in the molecule and in each cell.

Or maybe we will discover the unified illumination, the laws of the X factor of knowledge, the eternal dimension and the divine reality. What if we witness a cheeky Fibonacci sequence in nature, in the stock market or in music, or what if we meet the Self or the self? Why do they speak to us? What if we run into the other? Why do they seem familiar?

Or maybe there is no other.

'You are the divinity you seek.' I know I repeatedly said as much in the pages ahead, but unfortunately you are also the other you despise when you consign to oblivion your true nature. When you destroy nature, when you go against humanity, when you seek to demolish the divine civilization crafted from the sweat and blood of the shared, sacred ancestors. We are the other we detest when we traipse down the unnatural path of division, when we overlook the pure identity, misunderstand the fragile nature of life and upend everything and anything in our wake.

That is the other we must stand up against, not the one from another state, community or nation. That is the other who must evolve, the one who requires guidance, and the one who must be supported. The one with whom we must engage in dialogue and debate, build consensus and ensure cooperation and collaboration. This is as crystal clear as the cool waters of the Bhagirathi—or we can make it as bewildering as possible; for we are the creators of both the self and the other, of the now and the future, of the world and the universe.

As quantum beings, we can forge a new reality based on this understanding along with new connections and a new future. With quantum knowledge, with harmony, compassion, peace, wisdom and love, we can bask in the warm glow of pure vidya illuminating shared souls, shared dreams and shared progress.

Why make the 'other' choice literally?

The fruit of the tree of life is ripe for picking

With the exalted choice of Gyan Yoga, the intersection of quantum journeys and the cosmic truth will offer clarity, courage and direction. This will create questions and conversations, too. So, we must prepare for an ongoing cerebral quest, with the alchemy of the intellect and the soul where authenticity, abundance, awareness and acceptance will be a given. Acceptance not of injustice, bigotry, racism, discrimination, the growing inequalities or the moral vacuum in society, but of the flow of reality, the democratic embrace of wisdom, the truth of time and the circular nature of life.

As the Aham Brahmasmi principle, a luminous reality befitting our status—as the knowledge factor in motion, the Divinity Principle in play and the natural creator at work—is a distinct possibility. Remember we are a self-fulfilling prophecy aligned with excellence, innovation, mathematics, poetry, the matrix mind, art, beauty and nature.

With this singular reality and the grace of the eternal self, let's nurture the spiritual without the superstition, divinity without dogma, peace without polarization, belief without bigotry, enthusiasm without extremism and illumination without illusion.

Let the sacred light of knowledge illuminate the blessed journey from ignorance towards Absolute knowledge and Eternal truth, to the sacred one who is the bestower of abundance and cosmic bliss, to the generous source of eternity and authenticity, to the merciful one who accepts, heals and embraces, to the source of immortality, to the source of everything.

Asto ma sadgamaya
Tamso ma jyotirgamaya
Mrityor ma amritamgamaya
Om shanti, shanti, shanti
(Brahadaranyaka Upanishad)

Lead me from illusion to truth
Lead me from darkness to light
Lead me from death to immortality
Peace, peace and peace.